MAKER

CREATE A COSTUME!

COMICS

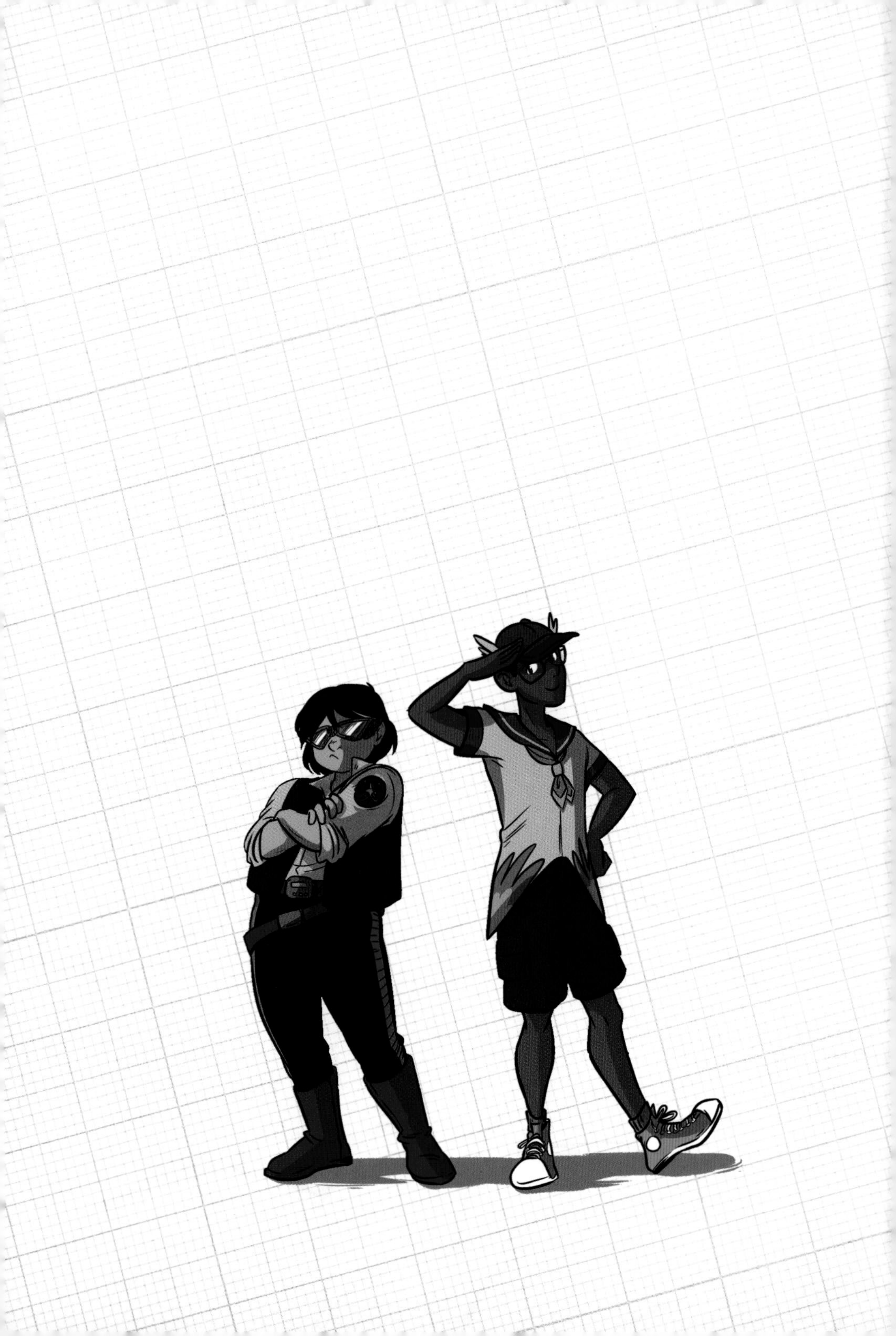

# CREATE A COSTUME!

### Sarah Myer

:01
First Second
New York

Making your own costumes is exciting, but it can be all too easy to lose sight of safety while you're sewing and crafting away!

Keep a close eye on your pins, needles, scissors, seam ripper, and other sharp objects while you are working. Place pins and needles in a pincushion for safekeeping when they are not in use.

Watch your hands when using a hot iron or hot glue gun, and never leave those tools unattended. Unplug all of your equipment when you're finished! Read your instruction manual and don't hesitate to ask for help before using a sewing machine. Keep your fingers away from the moving parts of the sewing machine and take your time.

Some paint and glue give off hazardous fumes and require proper ventilation. Read the labels and heed any warnings before you set up your work areas. Always keep your work area tidy to avoid accidents, and clean up after each stage of your project.

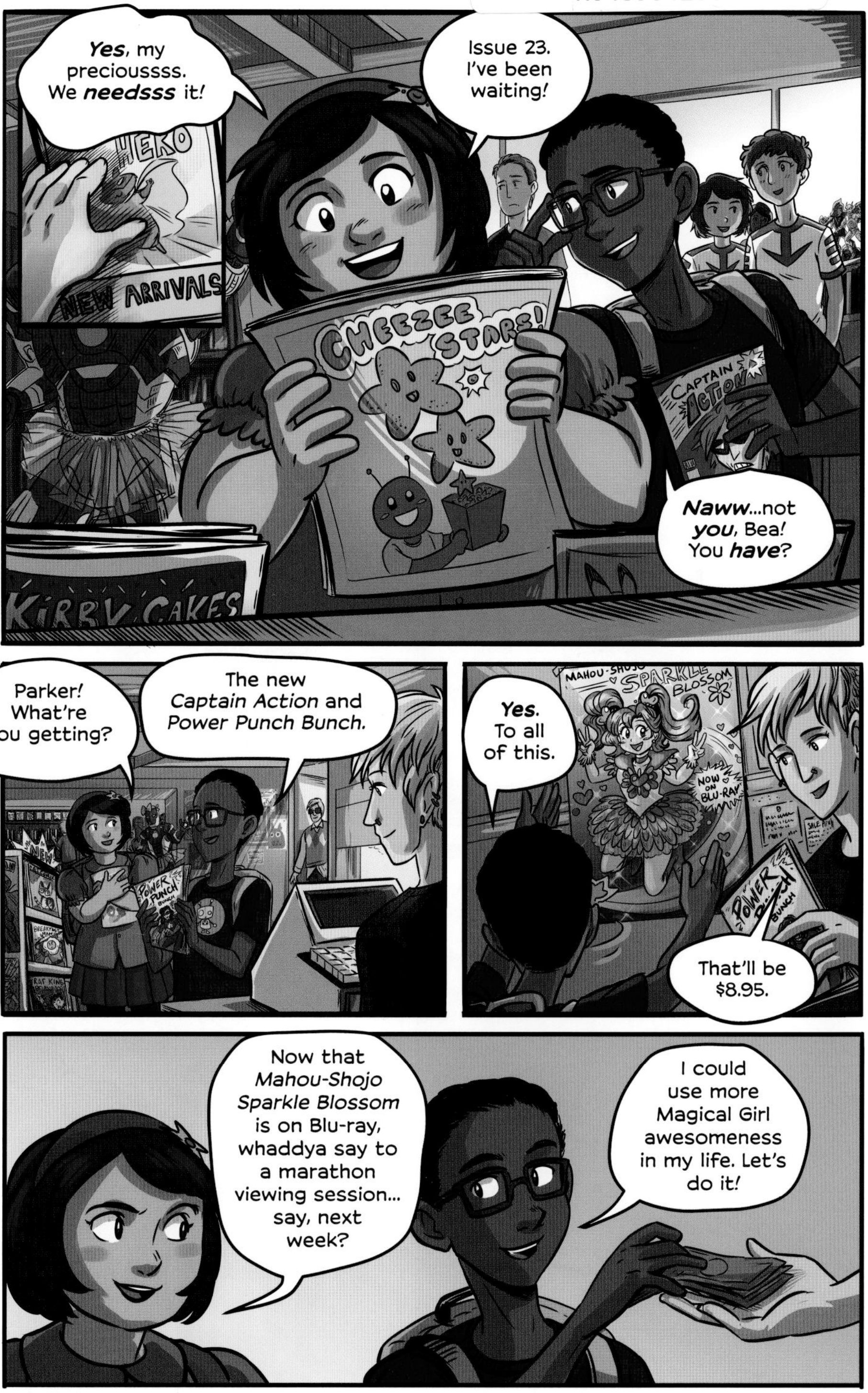
Yes, my preciousssss. We needsss it!
HERO
NEW ARRIVALS
Issue 23. I've been waiting!
CHEEZEE STARS!
CAPTAIN ACTION
Naww...not you, Bea! You have?
KIRBY CAKES
Parker! What're you getting?
The new Captain Action and Power Punch Bunch.
POWER PUNCH BUNCH
MAHOU-SHOJO SPARKLE BLOSSOM
NOW ON BLU-RAY
Yes. To all of this.
That'll be $8.95.
Now that Mahou-Shojo Sparkle Blossom is on Blu-ray, whaddya say to a marathon viewing session... say, next week?
I could use more Magical Girl awesomeness in my life. Let's do it!

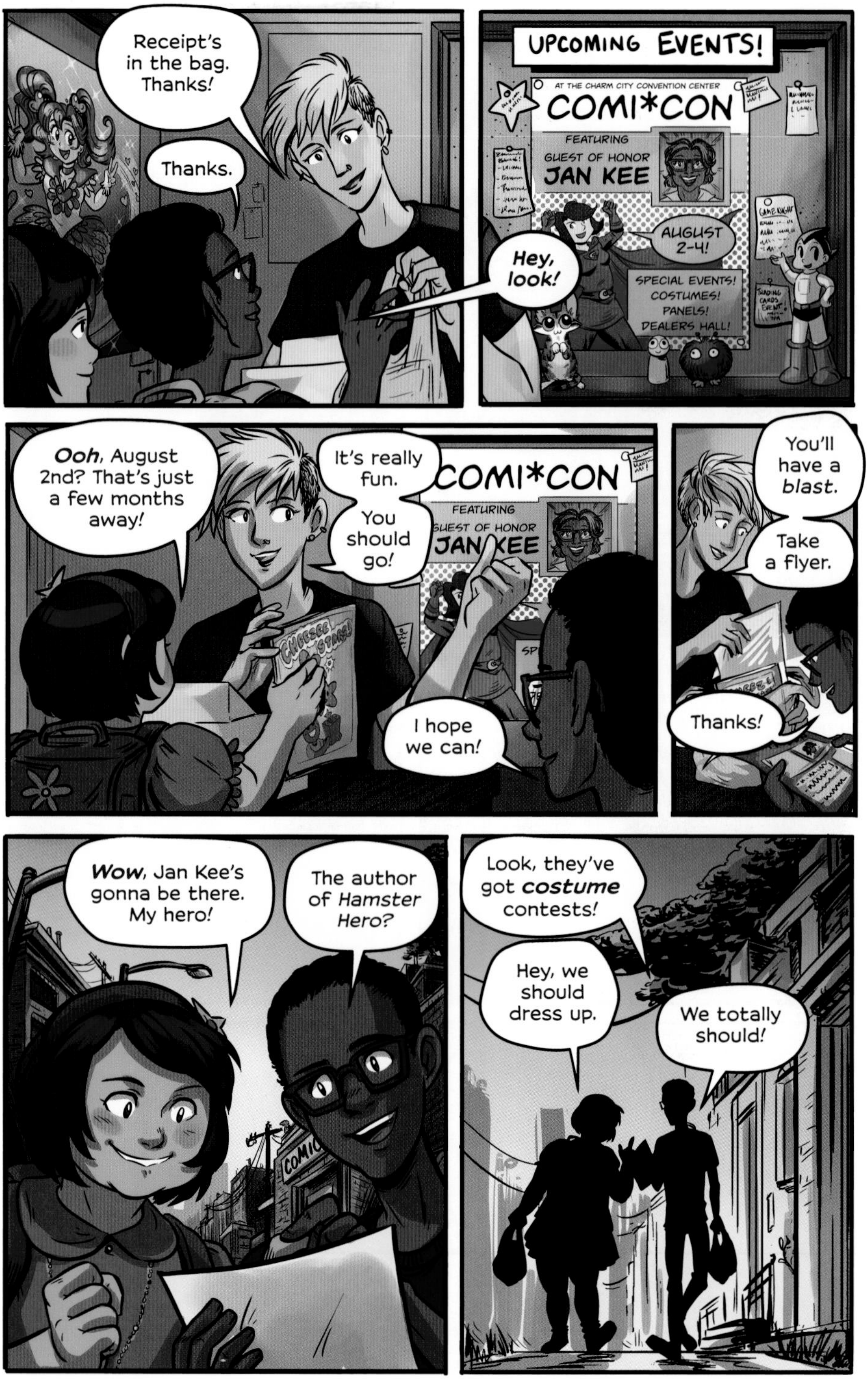
Receipt's in the bag. Thanks!
Thanks.
UPCOMING EVENTS!
AT THE CHARM CITY CONVENTION CENTER
COMI*CON
FEATURING
GUEST OF HONOR
JAN KEE
AUGUST 2-4!
SPECIAL EVENTS! COSTUMES! PANELS! DEALERS HALL!
Hey, look!
Ooh, August 2nd? That's just a few months away!
It's really fun.
You should go!
I hope we can!
You'll have a blast.
Take a flyer.
Thanks!
Wow, Jan Kee's gonna be there. My hero!
The author of Hamster Hero?
Look, they've got costume contests!
Hey, we should dress up.
We totally should!

...And y'know that the costumes we helped make for *You're a Good Man, Charlie Brown* were on point.

Bea, you say that about *every* school play.

*Because it's true.* Every play. Every time.

What am I gonna do with you?

...But I do want to dress up for the con.

It would be the best thing ever. And...

...imagine being in *costume* at such a big event!

TWITCH

Maybe... but who should we cosplay* as?

Hehehe...

Hold that thought! I have urgent business...

*Cosplay: "costume" + "play"—to dress up like a character from pop culture.

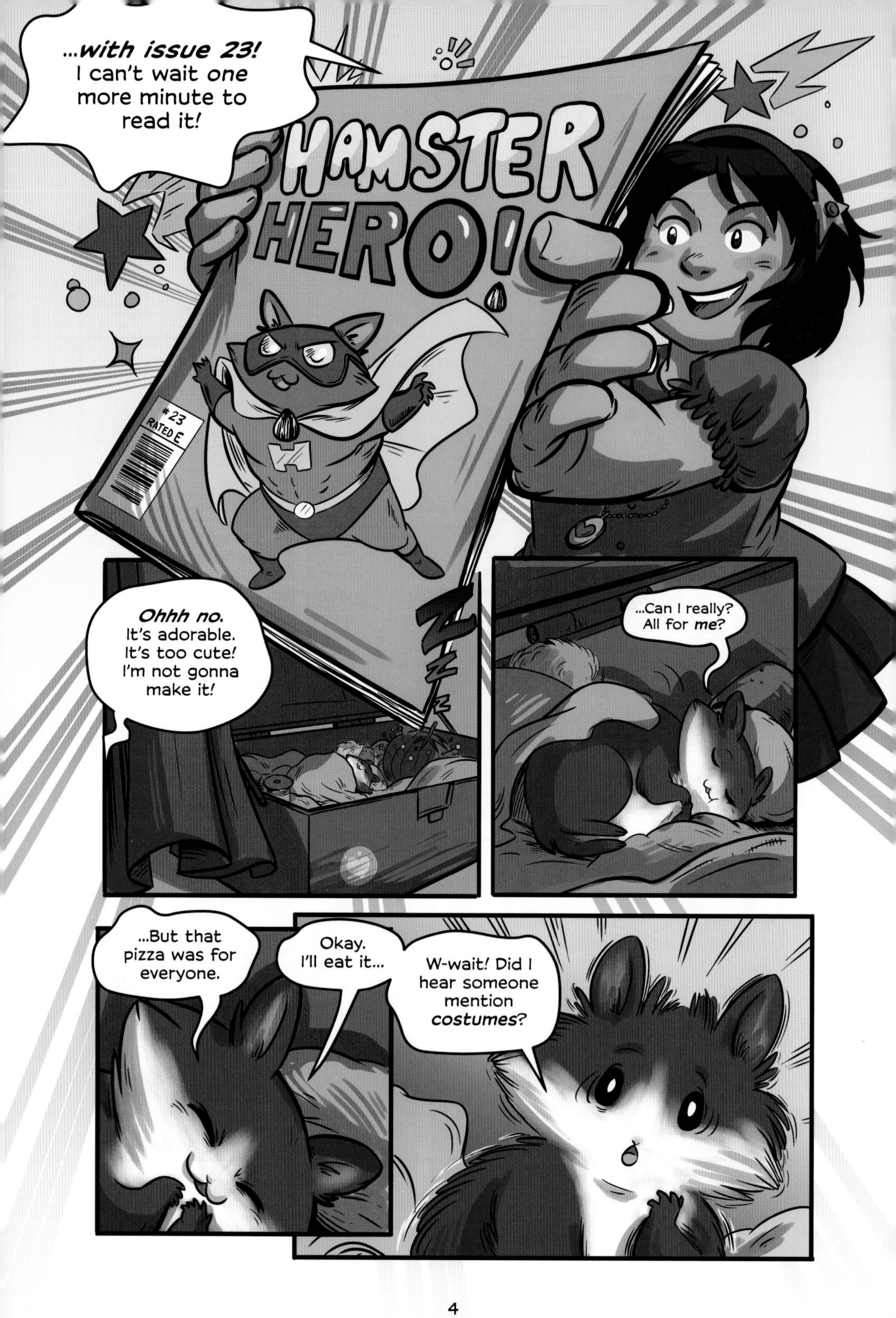
...with issue 23! I can't wait one more minute to read it!
HAMSTER HERO!
#23 RATED E
Ohhh no. It's adorable. It's too cute! I'm not gonna make it!
...Can I really? All for me?
...But that pizza was for everyone.
Okay. I'll eat it...
W-wait! Did I hear someone mention costumes?

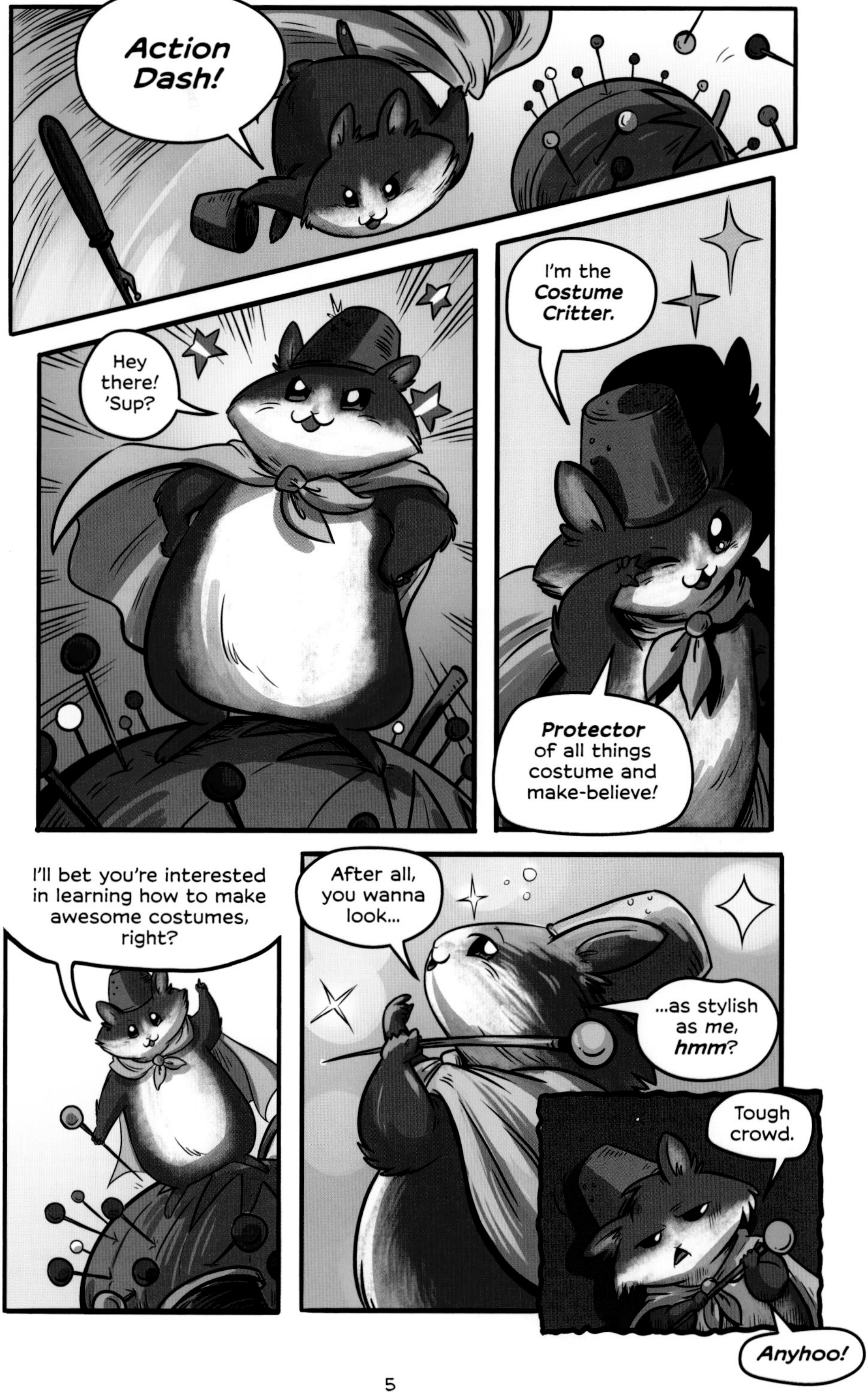
Action Dash!
Hey there! 'Sup?
I'm the Costume Critter.
Protector of all things costume and make-believe!
I'll bet you're interested in learning how to make awesome costumes, right?
After all, you wanna look...
...as stylish as me, hmm?
Tough crowd.
Anyhoo!

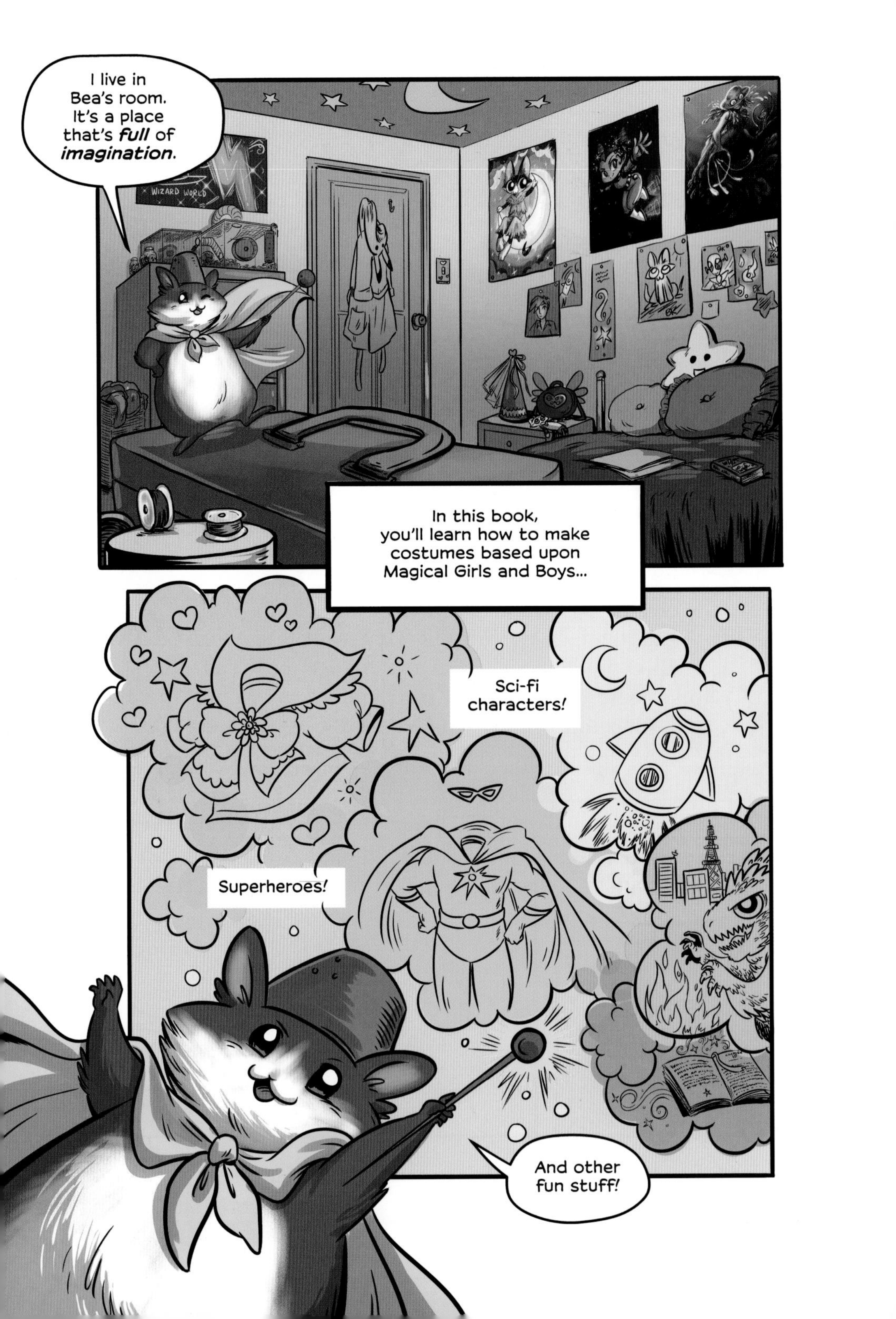

I live in Bea's room. It's a place that's *full* of ***imagination***.
WIZARD WORLD
In this book, you'll learn how to make costumes based upon Magical Girls and Boys...
Sci-fi characters!
Superheroes!
And other fun stuff!

What did she say?

Yes! My mom can give us a ride to the convention!

Maybe you want to go to a comic or anime convention...

or a Halloween or costume party. Either way, it's for *fun*!

I can't wait!

Same here!

So, let's get started on our costumes right now!

Hmmm, yeah, but... how?

...fabric and all brand-new materials...

For example, look at these two costumes.

*Super pricey!*
(from scratch)

*Just as super!*
(from recycled and modified clothes)

spandex: $10-$30 per yard

sewing pattern: $15-$25

total cost: $50-$150+

thrift store clothes: $5-$20 each

create your own design: $0

total cost: $15-$50+

Use old rain boots!

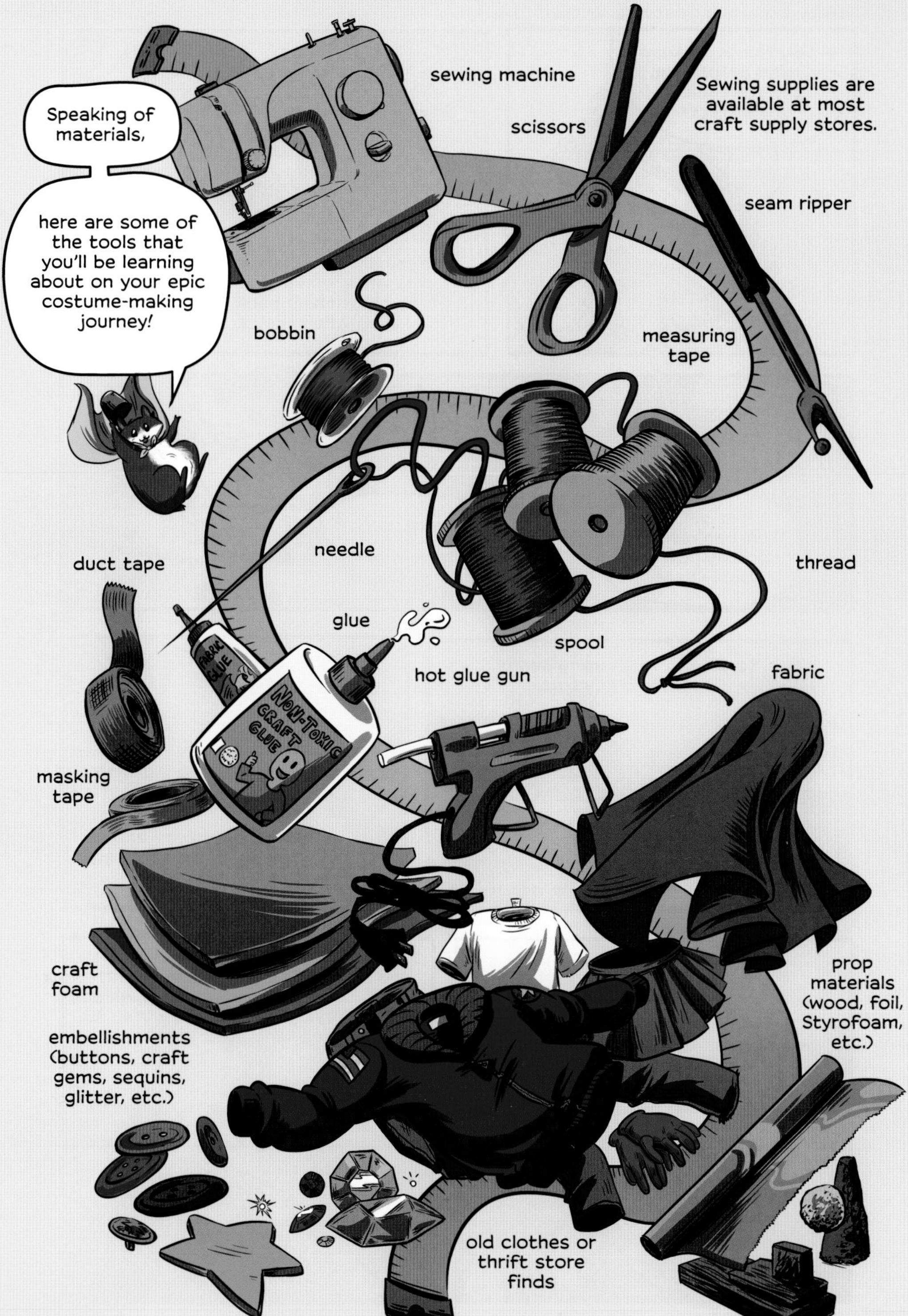
Speaking of materials,
here are some of the tools that you'll be learning about on your epic costume-making journey!
sewing machine
scissors
Sewing supplies are available at most craft supply stores.
seam ripper
bobbin
measuring tape
needle
duct tape
thread
glue
spool
hot glue gun
fabric
FABRIC GLUE
NON-TOXIC CRAFT GLUE
masking tape
craft foam
prop materials (wood, foil, Styrofoam, etc.)
embellishments (buttons, craft gems, sequins, glitter, etc.)
old clothes or thrift store finds

Safety tips with Costume Critter!

A few things to keep in mind before you get started on any project!

First!

Be mindful of where you place your pins while working, and remember to place them back in the pincushion when they aren't in use!

A lost pin is no fun, because it's gotta show up somewhere...

*eventually.*

Be careful when using seam rippers and scissors.

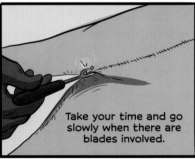

Take your time and go slowly when there are blades involved.

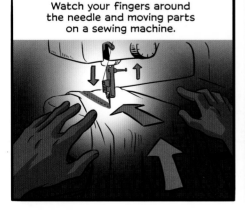

Watch your fingers around the needle and moving parts on a sewing machine.

Mind the warnings on glues and adhesives before working with them. Some emit toxic fumes while curing (drying). Be sure to work in a well-ventilated area!

Safety while wearing the costume is important to consider, too.

Check the fit of the costume often...

Yaaaaay!

...so that you are comfortable while wearing it...

Owowow owowow owowow owowow owow!

...for as long as you need.

Regrets. I got 'em.

I am *Night Cat! I fear nothing!*

While you're wearing a hat, mask, or helmet...

...visibility is important.

BONK

DEALER HALL LINE STARTS
THIS WAY
FRI 12-8 PM
SAT 10-6 PM
SUN 10-3 PM

Sand down any pointy or sharp parts on wooden props.

WHOA!

Sandpaper →

Even after sanding, use caution when handling your props!

When in doubt, ask someone more experienced for help!

Ah, these outfits are *so cool!*

How do you think she gets her hair to stay like that?

Uhh... magical *hairspray?*

Y'think *we* could make these costumes?

We've got the tools right here!

Let's give it a try!

*Yeah, I'm in!*

Ooh, hey! It looks like we've already got our very first project!

TRANSFORM! MAGICAL GIRL (AND BOY!) COSTUME

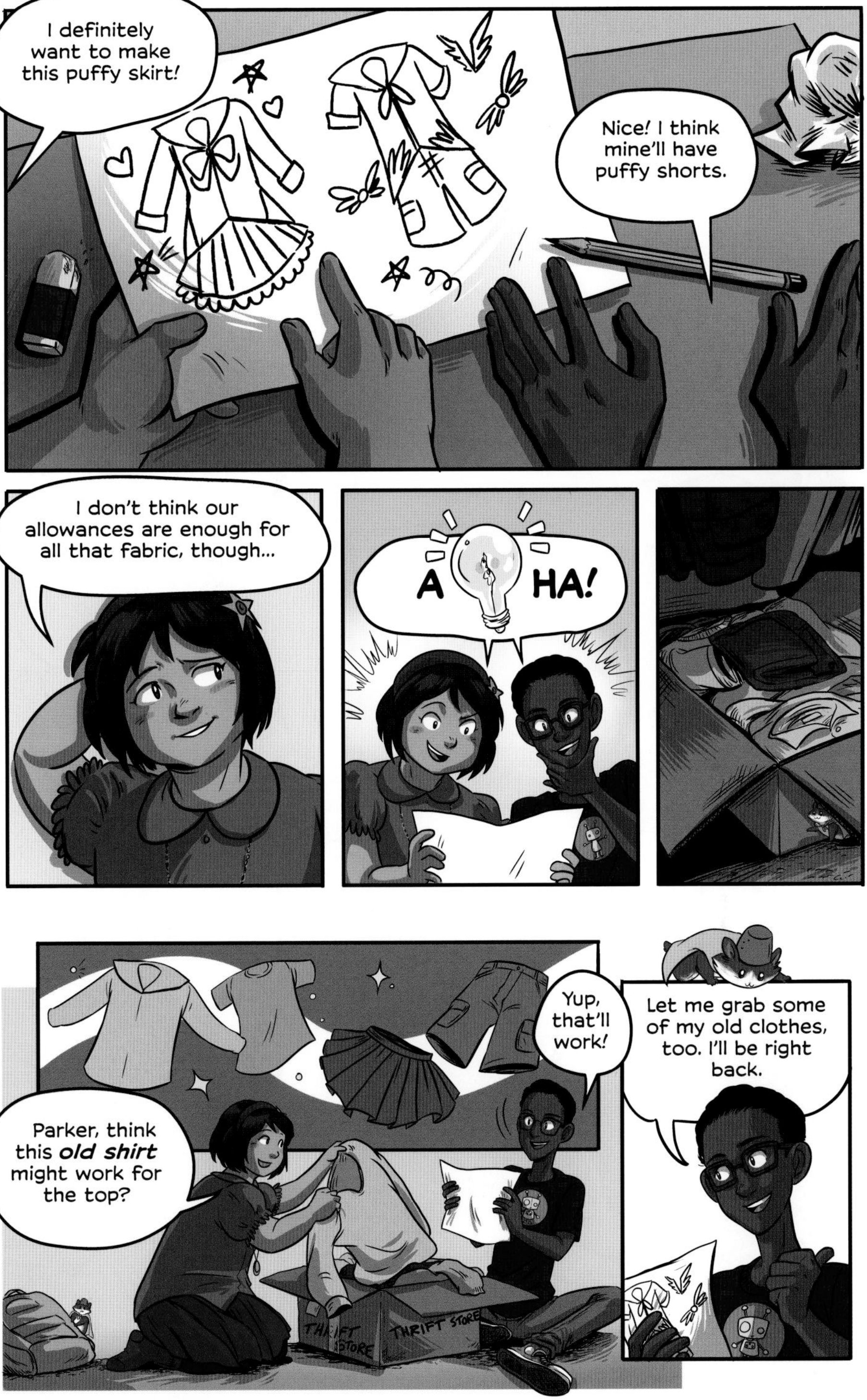
I definitely want to make this puffy skirt!
Nice! I think mine'll have puffy shorts.
I don't think our allowances are enough for all that fabric, though...
A HA!
Parker, think this ***old shirt*** might work for the top?
THRIFT STORE
THRIFT STORE
Yup, that'll work!
Let me grab some of my old clothes, too. I'll be right back.

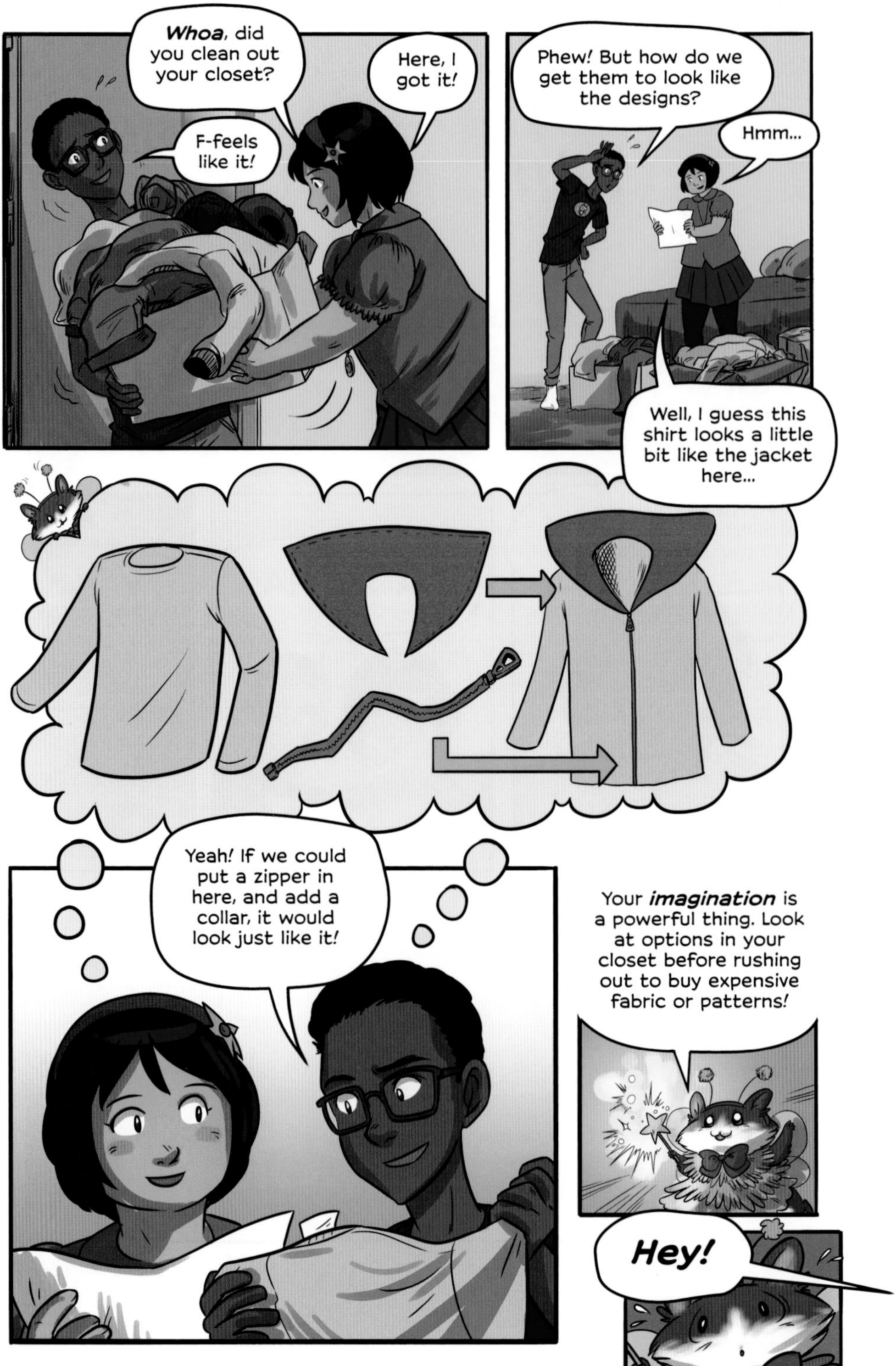
*Whoa*, did you clean out your closet?
F-feels like it!
Here, I got it!
Phew! But how do we get them to look like the designs?
Hmm...
Well, I guess this shirt looks a little bit like the jacket here...
Yeah! If we could put a zipper in here, and add a collar, it would look just like it!
Your *imagination* is a powerful thing. Look at options in your closet before rushing out to buy expensive fabric or patterns!
Hey!

Look at your design and think about what could
be added or subtracted to the existing clothing
in order to match the design.

We'll be using a sewing machine for these costumes.
Don't worry—it's easier than you think!

First, prepare the shirt!

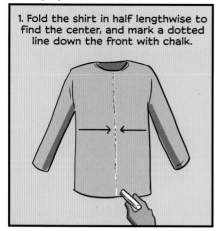

1. Fold the shirt in half lengthwise to find the center, and mark a dotted line down the front with chalk.

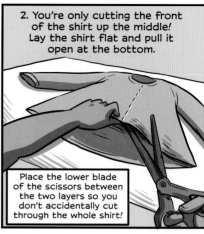

2. You're only cutting the front of the shirt up the middle! Lay the shirt flat and pull it open at the bottom.

Place the lower blade of the scissors between the two layers so you don't accidentally cut through the whole shirt!

Keep this hand free of the scissors' path!

Rest your cutting hand flat as you cut!

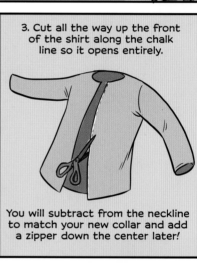

3. Cut all the way up the front of the shirt along the chalk line so it opens entirely.

You will subtract from the neckline to match your new collar and add a zipper down the center later!

Tip: Make sure you always cut fabric with *fabric* scissors. Don't use paper or craft scissors, as they aren't sharp enough to cut fabric cleanly and safely. Use a cutting mat to protect your work surfaces.

Next, let's make a simple paper pattern for a sailor collar!

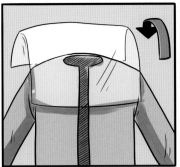

**1.** Fold tracing or parchment paper over the top of your shirt.

**2.** Draw the shape of your collar with chalk on the paper.

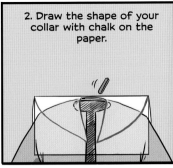

**3.** Repeat for the back.

**4.** Lay the paper flat and cut!

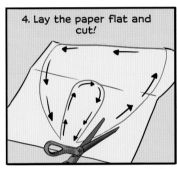

Now you've got your very own sailor collar pattern!

Lay the sailor collar pattern on top of your shirt and trace around the edges where they lay over the center of the shirt.

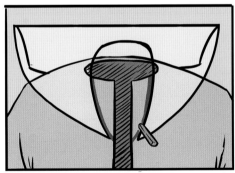

Cut the shirt collar along the chalk lines, so that your shirt won't show behind the collar later.

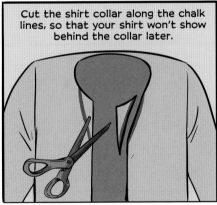

Tracing or parchment paper is perfect because it's see-through!

The next step is using the paper pattern to cut out the same shape from fabric.

Sewing fabric requires an understanding of the "right" and "wrong" sides of the fabric. You want to sew fabric pieces together so that the "right" side is outside on the final product and all of the seams end up tucked inside facing the "wrong" side. To do this, many projects require you to sew fabric pieces "wrong" side out at first.

Here's how to determine the "right" and "wrong" sides of fabric. Look at the *selvage** along the edge of the fabric.

See the holes? If they are *raised* slightly, then you are looking at the "right" side of the fabric.

Now sew your collar!

1. Fold your fabric in half with the right side facing in. Trace around your pattern with chalk on the wrong side (facing out).

selvage

2. Cut out your fabric collar through both layers, about 1/2" outside the chalk.

Now you've got two collar pieces!

right side

wrong side

3. Put the pieces together, with the right sides of the fabric facing each other.

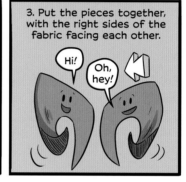

Hi!

Oh, hey!

Think of it as a fabric sandwich.

No filling in the sandwich?

Yeah, where's the beef?

Now it's time to pin the two pieces of fabric together.

Remember to keep your pins in your pincushion when they aren't in use!

The pin enters the fabric at one point here and the sharp end comes out the other side.

Like so!

Continue pinning all the way around the edges of the fabric.

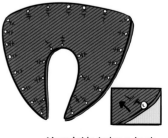

Now let's take a look at the sewing machine.

*For more information, look at the glossary on page 122.

## Anatomy of a Sewing Machine

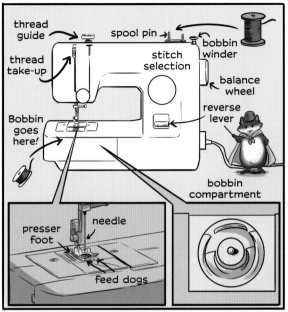

thread guide

spool pin

bobbin winder

thread take-up

stitch selection

balance wheel

reverse lever

Bobbin goes here!

bobbin compartment

presser foot

needle

feed dogs

Your sewing machine may look different! You should always keep and consult the machine instruction manual.

INSTRUCTION MANUAL

I shall bask in its guiding light!

To thread the machine:

1. Pull the thread over to the thread guide.

2. Bring the thread down, around, and up to the thread take-up.

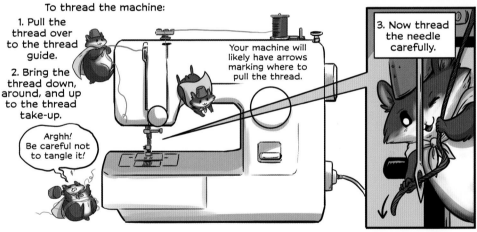

Your machine will likely have arrows marking where to pull the thread.

Arghh! Be careful not to tangle it!

3. Now thread the needle carefully.

The thread goes through the front of the needle...

...into the foot and out the side.

Place the filled bobbin into the bobbin compartment.

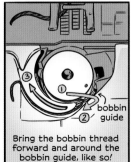

bobbin guide

Bring the bobbin thread forward and around the bobbin guide, like so!

19

Now pull the needle thread up and away from the machine so it's taut.

Turn the balance wheel counter-clockwise to push the needle down. ×1

The needle picks up the bobbin thread.

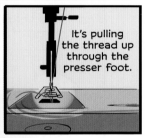

It's pulling the thread up through the presser foot.

Pull both threads back, under the foot and behind the machine.

Close the bobbin feed door.

Okay! Now you're ready to start sewing!

Place the tip of your collar under the foot of the machine about an inch or so from the point.

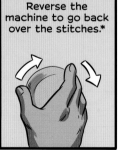

presser foot

Push the lever next to the needle down to hold the fabric in place.

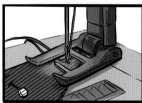

Gently press down on the pedal to sew a few stitches and then stop.

Reverse the machine to go back over the stitches.*

*Check your sewing machine manual for instructions.

This reinforces the stitches and ensures they won't come loose! You'll do the same when you finish.

Sew back over the stitches 1" to secure them!

Sew around the outside edge of the collar about 1/2" from the edge, stopping to remove pins before the needle gets to them.

Cut the loose thread, remove any pins you missed, and turn the collar right side out.

Push the corners out with your fingers. A pen or chopstick works well, too!

Nice and pointy!

On a low setting, iron the collar to press the seams flat.

Careful, it's hot!

Place the collar inside the shirt so that it is upside down. Match the neck hole of the collar to the shirt.

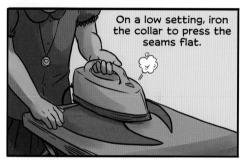

Pin the collar along the shirt. Take your time!

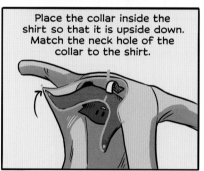

Make sure the ends of the collar are even!

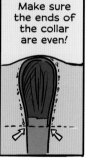

Measure from the bottom of the collar to the bottom hem of the shirt to determine what length zipper you will need.

Record the measurement so you can buy a zipper that fits!

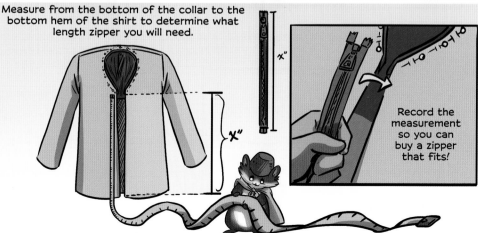

21

Let's take a closer look at how the zipper and collar should look when they're sewn properly in place!

The fabric is hiding the seam because the seam is underneath, and the fabric is folded under! Smooth!

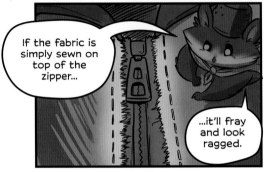

If the fabric is simply sewn on top of the zipper...

...it'll fray and look ragged.

Here's a cross section of what the seam looks like.

To pin your zipper, flip it over against the left side of the shirt, so the front of the zipper is facing down.

Pin the zipper to the jacket.

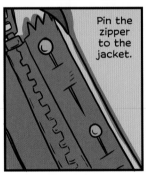

Now flip the zipper and pin the top to hold it in place.

Unzip the zipper...

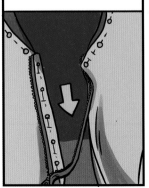

...and pin the other side of the zipper to the other side of the shirt, with the teeth facing away from the center.

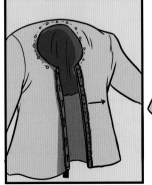

Now sew the collar...

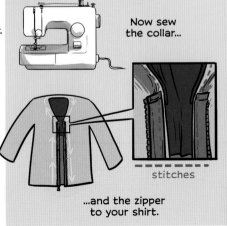

- - - - - - - -
stitches

...and the zipper to your shirt.

It's going to look weird at first.
Where's the collar supposed to be?

Pull the collar out and
over the top!

TA-DA!

You've come up against the sewing machine, the iron, pins, and the scissors!
You're on your way to becoming the *Costume-Making Champ!*

Now check the fit of the top.

You can use the same method you
used for the collar to add cuffs,
if you want.

Next, let's make some tails to give
the top some extra flair!

Lay the shirt on its side and measure across the bottom to determine the width of the top of your triangle shapes for the side tails.

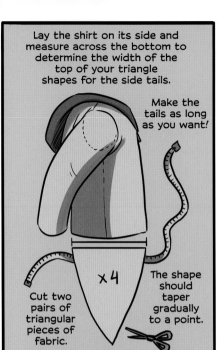

Make the tails as long as you want!

x 4

The shape should taper gradually to a point.

Cut two pairs of triangular pieces of fabric.

The triangles can be a different color of fabric if you'd like. Use what you have on hand if you can't afford fabric that matches the shirt.

You can decorate the tails later.

1. Pin each pair of tails together, right sides in, leaving the top of the triangle unpinned.

2. Sew each tail together about 1/2" in from the edges, leaving the top of the triangle open.

Tip: Snip the bottom tips of each triangle about 1/4" from the stitches before turning them out. This makes the tip extra pointy!

3. Turn each triangle right side out, gently pushing the tips outward.

4. Press flat with the iron.

5. Pin the tails to the outside of your shirt, as shown. (The tails will be upside down.)

6. Sew the tails to the shirt along the edges that you've pinned for each, leaving a 1/2" seam.

The seam between the tails and the bottom of the shirt is hidden on the inside of the costume.

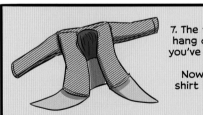

7. The tails should hang down when you've sewn them.

Now turn the shirt inside out!

8. Where the shirt and tail meet, lay the seam flat and iron it.

Adding the tails gives your costume a bit of flair, don't you think?

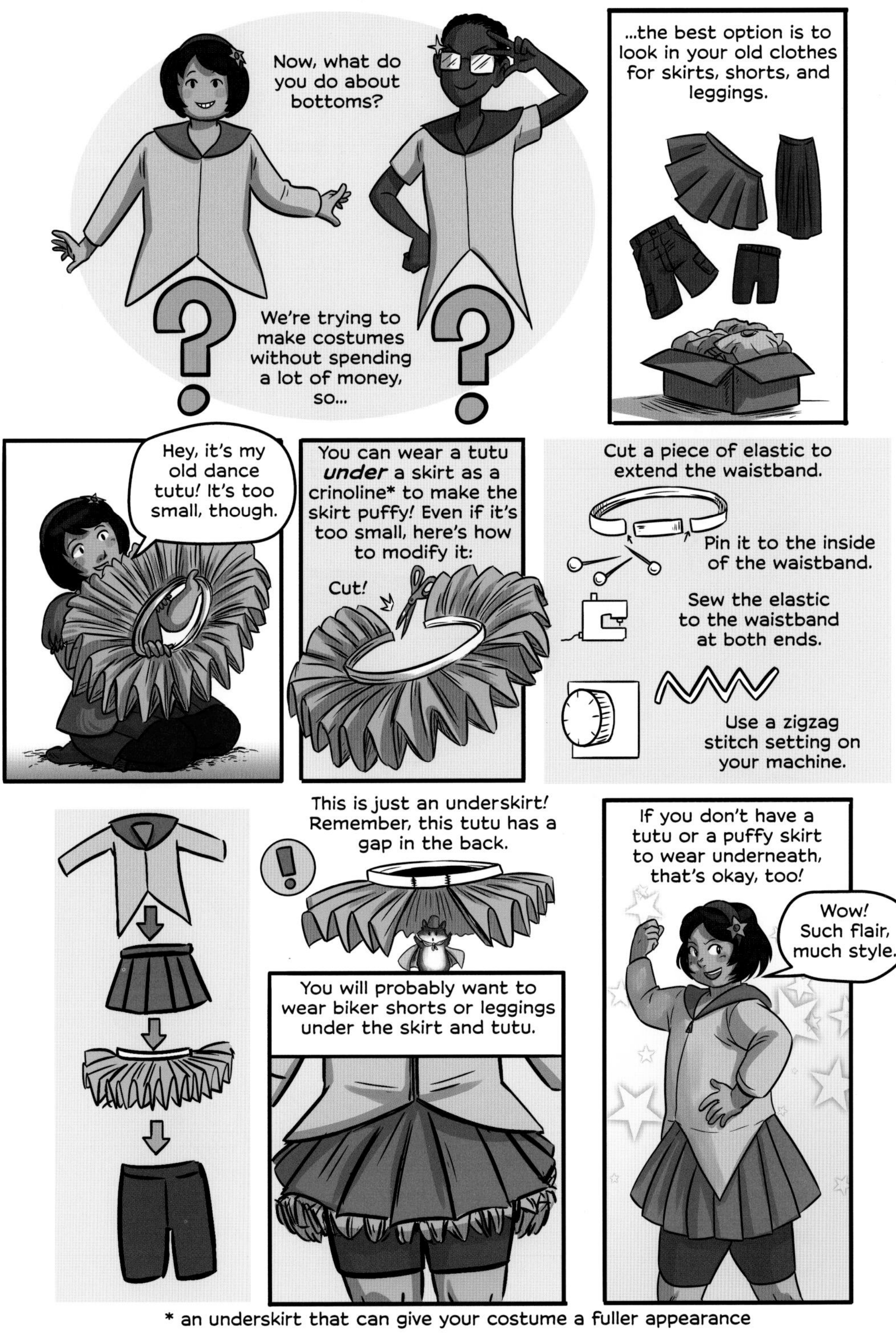
Now, what do you do about bottoms?
We're trying to make costumes without spending a lot of money, so...
...the best option is to look in your old clothes for skirts, shorts, and leggings.
Hey, it's my old dance tutu! It's too small, though.
You can wear a tutu *under* a skirt as a crinoline* to make the skirt puffy! Even if it's too small, here's how to modify it:
Cut!
Cut a piece of elastic to extend the waistband.
Pin it to the inside of the waistband.
Sew the elastic to the waistband at both ends.
Use a zigzag stitch setting on your machine.
This is just an underskirt! Remember, this tutu has a gap in the back.
You will probably want to wear biker shorts or leggings under the skirt and tutu.
If you don't have a tutu or a puffy skirt to wear underneath, that's okay, too!
Wow! Such flair, much style.

* an underskirt that can give your costume a fuller appearance

# Make It Magical!

Here are some ways to add some decorative touches to your costume.

fabric glue

hot glue gun

ribbon

bias tape*

Pin and sew ribbon or bias tape to the collar for stripe accents!

Embellishment ideas:

Glue craft gems and ribbon to a headband.

Cut shapes from colored felt or craft foam to add to your collar, skirt, shorts, or tails. Lots of Magical Girl or Boy characters have hearts, stars, and moon shapes all over their costumes.

craft foam

craft gems

*a narrow strip of fabric with an oblique, or slanted, fabric grain. Bias tape is more flexible than fabric with a grain that's parallel to the selvage. This flexibility makes it great for finishing the edges of fabric, like collars and hems.

Make your own sailor tie and bow!

Pointed at one end!

1. Cut four equally sized pieces of fabric for your tie measuring at least 8" long and one rectangular piece or wide ribbon for the "knot" or loop.

2. Following the same steps for the collar, pin, sew, turn out, and iron your tie and knot pieces.

3. Hand sew or use your machine to sew Velcro to the back of the collar and the top of your tie to hold it in place.

Velcro

You can use the same method to create a bow!

Cut shapes out of craft foam or felt, and glue them together to create brooches. Hot glue craft gems and pin backs.

pin back

You can put these brooches anywhere— even on a hat!

Customize the brooches to fit your character's personality!

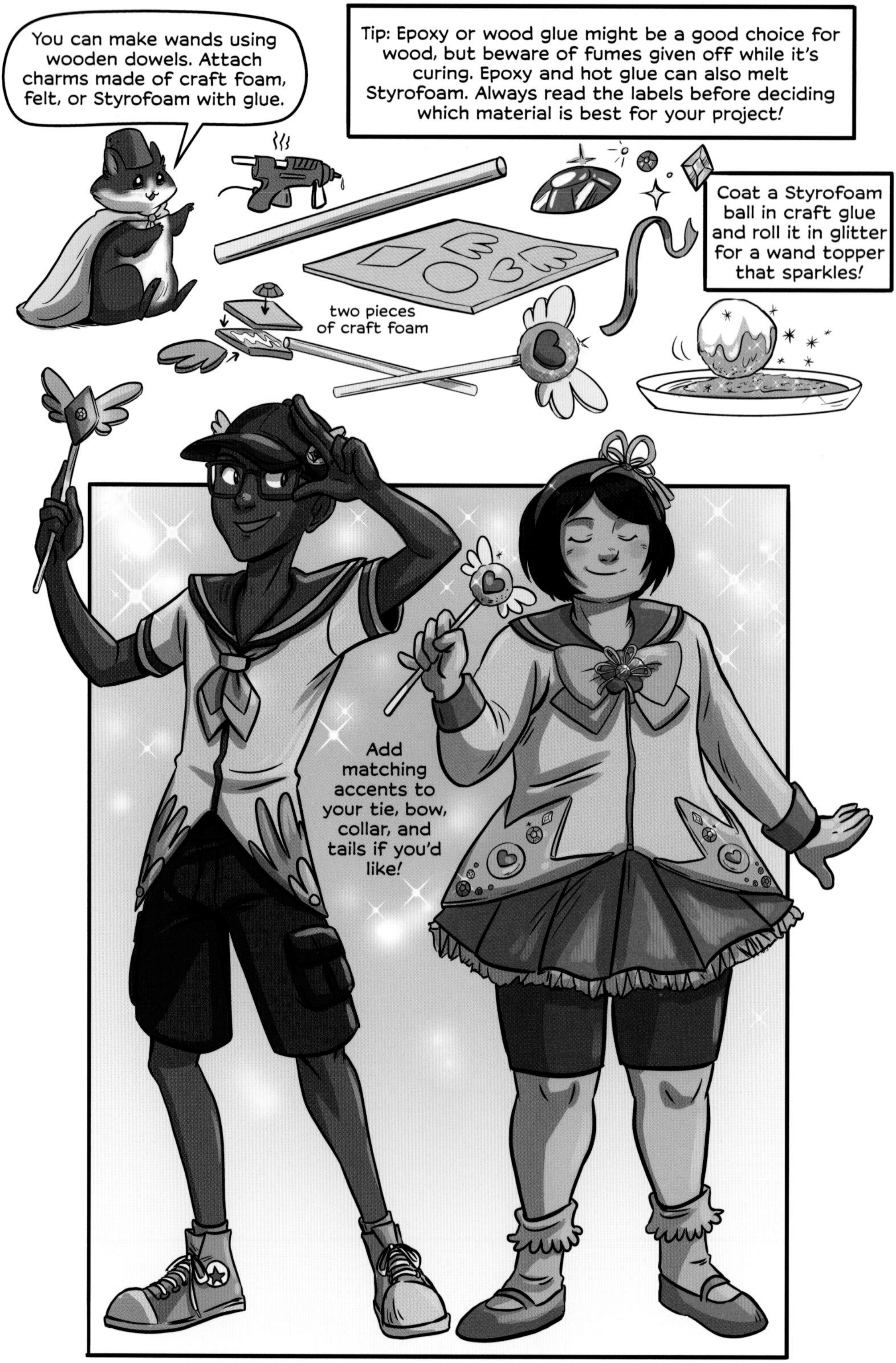

You can make wands using wooden dowels. Attach charms made of craft foam, felt, or Styrofoam with glue.
Tip: Epoxy or wood glue might be a good choice for wood, but beware of fumes given off while it's curing. Epoxy and hot glue can also melt Styrofoam. Always read the labels before deciding which material is best for your project!
Coat a Styrofoam ball in craft glue and roll it in glitter for a wand topper that sparkles!
two pieces of craft foam
Add matching accents to your tie, bow, collar, and tails if you'd like!

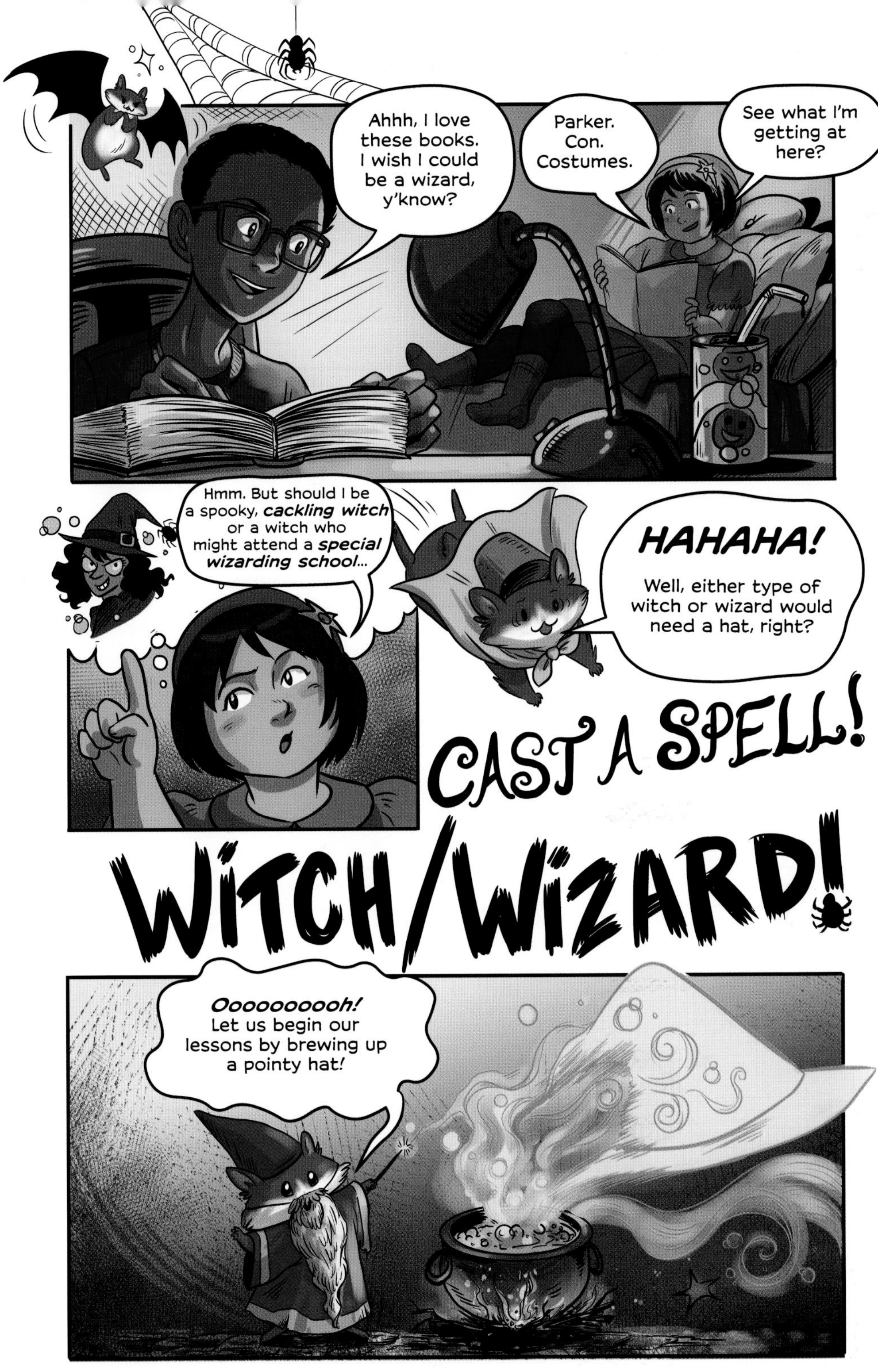
Ahhh, I love these books. I wish I could be a wizard, y'know?
Parker. Con. Costumes.
See what I'm getting at here?
Hmm. But should I be a spooky, *cackling witch* or a witch who might attend a *special wizarding school*...
*HAHAHA!*
Well, either type of witch or wizard would need a hat, right?
CAST A SPELL!
WITCH/WIZARD!
*Ooooooooooh!* Let us begin our lessons by brewing up a pointy hat*!*

Make a base for the hat!

cone

brim

Materials:
craft foam,
duct tape,
felt,
craft glue,
compass,
newspaper,
pencil,
string, pin,
paint, ribbon

Measure the circumference of your head
with a measuring tape.

(Circumference is the distance around your head.)

Don't pull the tape too tight!

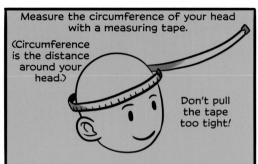

old newspaper       compass                    craft foam

duct tape

Let's say that your head measures 20" in circumference.

20" c

$\frac{?}{\pi}$   r

To draw the circle for your pattern evenly, you'll need to do a little math magic. In this instance:

c = circumference

r = radius (the distance from the center of the circle to the edge)

π (Pi) = 3.14

This is our magic formula!

$r = c/2\pi$

(or circumference ÷ 2π = radius)

c = 20
2π = 2 x 3.14 = 6.28
r = ?
Plug in the numbers!

20 ÷ 6.28 = 3.1847133758
Or, the radius is roughly 3.18 inches!

Confused?
Do an internet search for "circle calculator" and check your work.

Now you know to set your compass to this measurement.

3.18"

Use your compass to draw a circle for your head onto the newspaper. Now you'll need to draw another circle for the brim with a radius that's 4" longer. That's too big for your compass, but you can use a piece of string, a pin, and a pencil.

Pin

4"

Keep the string taut!

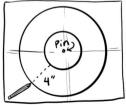

Fold the newspaper with your brim pattern in half to cut the pattern out.

Use the pattern to cut a brim from craft foam.*

Now make the cone from a craft foam piece. Add an extra inch to the circumference measurement from before to determine the length of the craft foam–i.e., 20" becomes 21". It should be 14" wide.

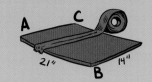

1. Bring point A and point B of the craft foam together so that A is overlapping B and the corners line up, as shown. Secure the tip where A and B meet with a small piece of duct tape.

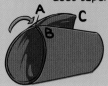

*You may need to tape a few pieces of craft foam together to get pieces large enough for the brim and the cone. Duct tape the front and back of the craft foam together along the seams.

2. Roll point C over the outside of the cone, tightening the shape inside the foam.

3. Continue to tighten the tip of the cone by bringing point C all the way around the outside until the end of the cone is rolled as tightly as it will go. Secure the outside seam and point C to the cone with duct tape. If it's too small for your head, make some small vertical cuts in the base.

view looking inside the cone

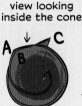

You'll cover the hat later, hiding the foam.

The cone should look like this when it is complete!

side

A-B

front

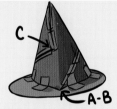

Now set the cone on top of the brim and secure with duct tape all the way around the edges and inside to reinforce the seam where the two pieces meet.

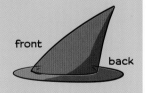

front

back

The extra craft foam layers rolled into the end of the cone will help make the tip of the hat sturdy during the next step...

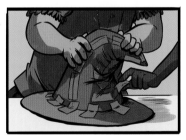

...which is to bend the hat at the tip toward the back and duct tape it in place to make the shape more interesting.

Witch and wizard hats can have all kinds of gnarly shapes! Twist it to make it narrower or fold it to create a crooked shape, securing the foam with duct tape as you work. You can even add a longer tip with scraps of craft foam!

Twist it!

Lay down some newspaper.
Cut pieces of felt and glue them to your hat with craft glue.

Let it dry overnight!

Trim off excess felt once the hat has dried.

You can paint your hat with acrylic paint over the felt to give it a leathery texture.

Add a ribbon and craft foam buckle if you'd like!

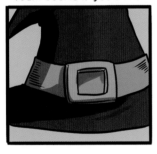

Cut shapes out of craft foam or felt to glue to your hat, or add some fake spiders!

Use a hole punch tool...

...and a bit of string to hang charms from your hat.

Now for the robe!

You will need a piece of fabric that is wide enough to reach from wrist to wrist across and, when folded in half, is tall enough to reach from your neck to your ankles.

FYI—You're basically making a T-shaped robe, with the bottom flaring out slightly!

1. Fold the fabric in half horizontally (across the height of the fabric) and lay down on it.

2. Have a friend mark lines for large, loose sleeves and leave a lot of room around your body.

3. Cut a triangular opening in the center of the fabric, large enough for your head to fit through, and drape the robe over your head.

4. Pin along the chalk lines. Having a friend to help with this while you are wearing it helps to ensure that the robes fit.

5. Remove the robe and cut about 1" outside the chalk lines for seam allowance.

Unpin the robe and flip it open.

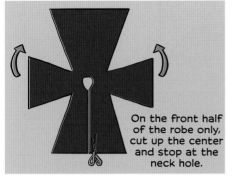

On the front half of the robe only, cut up the center and stop at the neck hole.

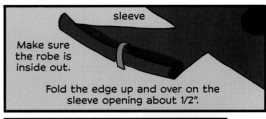

sleeve

Make sure the robe is inside out.

Fold the edge up and over on the sleeve opening about 1/2".

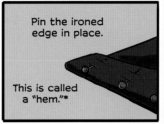

Repeat a second time.

Iron to press it flat.

Pin the ironed edge in place.

This is called a "hem."*

Repeat for all of the highlighted edges.

Sew your pinned edges. Begin and end with reverse stitching, and remove pins as you go. Check page 20 for instructions.

Iron and press the sewn edges flat.

Keeping the robe inside out, fold it so the front and back meet and pin the halves together along the edges you cut before, as shown in the next panel.

Pin the outside edges together.

Sew and iron!

To finish the collar of your robe, pin colored bias tape along the edge of the collar and down the front of the robe. Then sew it in place!

Fold the bias tape around the robe fabric as you secure it with the pins.

* See glossary on page 122.

Sew a ribbon or bias tape pieces to the inside of your robe.

This way, you can tie it closed at the collar!

Cut decorative shapes out of felt or craft foam.

Attach them with fabric glue.

You can also make your own patches! Here's how.

1. Draw your design in pencil on some white or pale fabric.

2. Paint the design using acrylic paint.

Tip: Painting to the edge of the design keeps the fabric from fraying when you cut!

3. Let it dry!

4. Cut out the design.

Glue or sew the patch to your robe.

*Yeehehee, I'm feelin' spooky.*

Mwahaha!

Oh! Waitasec!

We don't have any wands!

Look outside for sticks!

Dry, dead branches make the best wands!

Wipe off any dirt or grime with a rag.

Using sandpaper on a work surface, carefully rub the rougher bits of bark off to smooth it down and get rid of extra grime.

All clean!

air-dry clay

craft or wood glue

NON-TOXIC CRAFT GLUE

Apply a little glue to the end of the stick where the handle will go.

Use the air-dry clay to mold a handle around the end over the glue.

Let it dry!

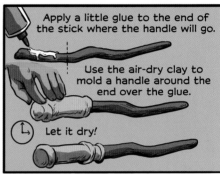

Paint the wand! You can water down acrylic paint for a wood stain effect, too!

Add feathers, glitter, craft gems, or whatever else you can think of!

Here are some ideas for custom wand decorations!

Put some glue on the tip of the wand...

...and roll it in glitter!

Glue fake spiders to the end!

feathers

craft gem

twine or yarn

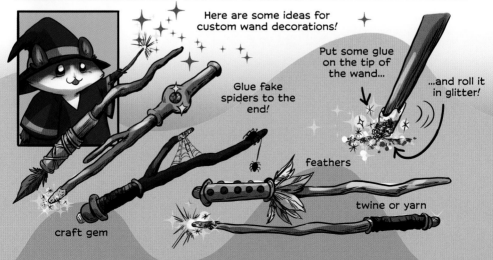

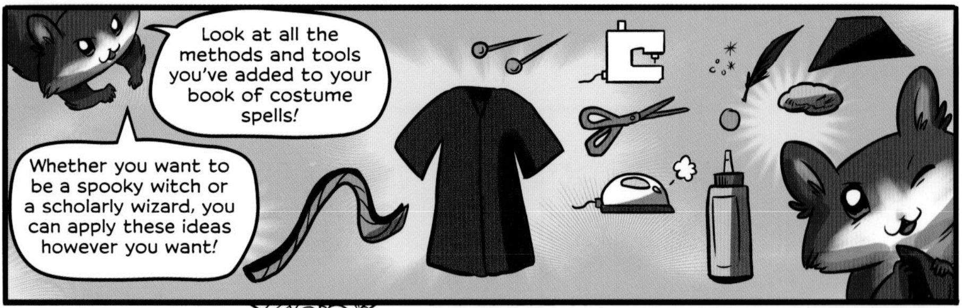
Look at all the methods and tools you've added to your book of costume spells!
Whether you want to be a spooky witch or a scholarly wizard, you can apply these ideas however you want!

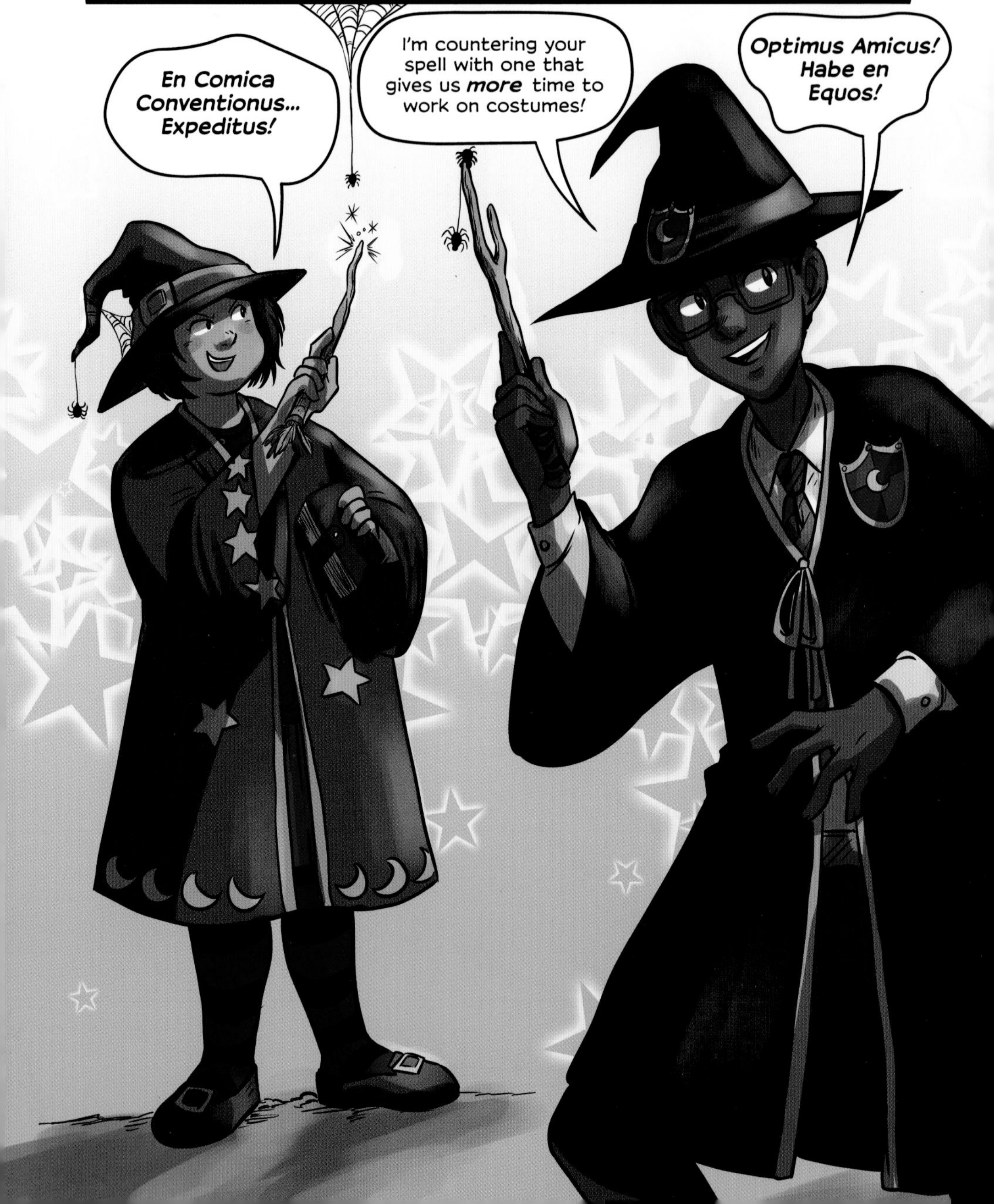
En Comica Conventionus... Expeditus!
I'm countering your spell with one that gives us *more* time to work on costumes!
Optimus Amicus! Habe en Equos!

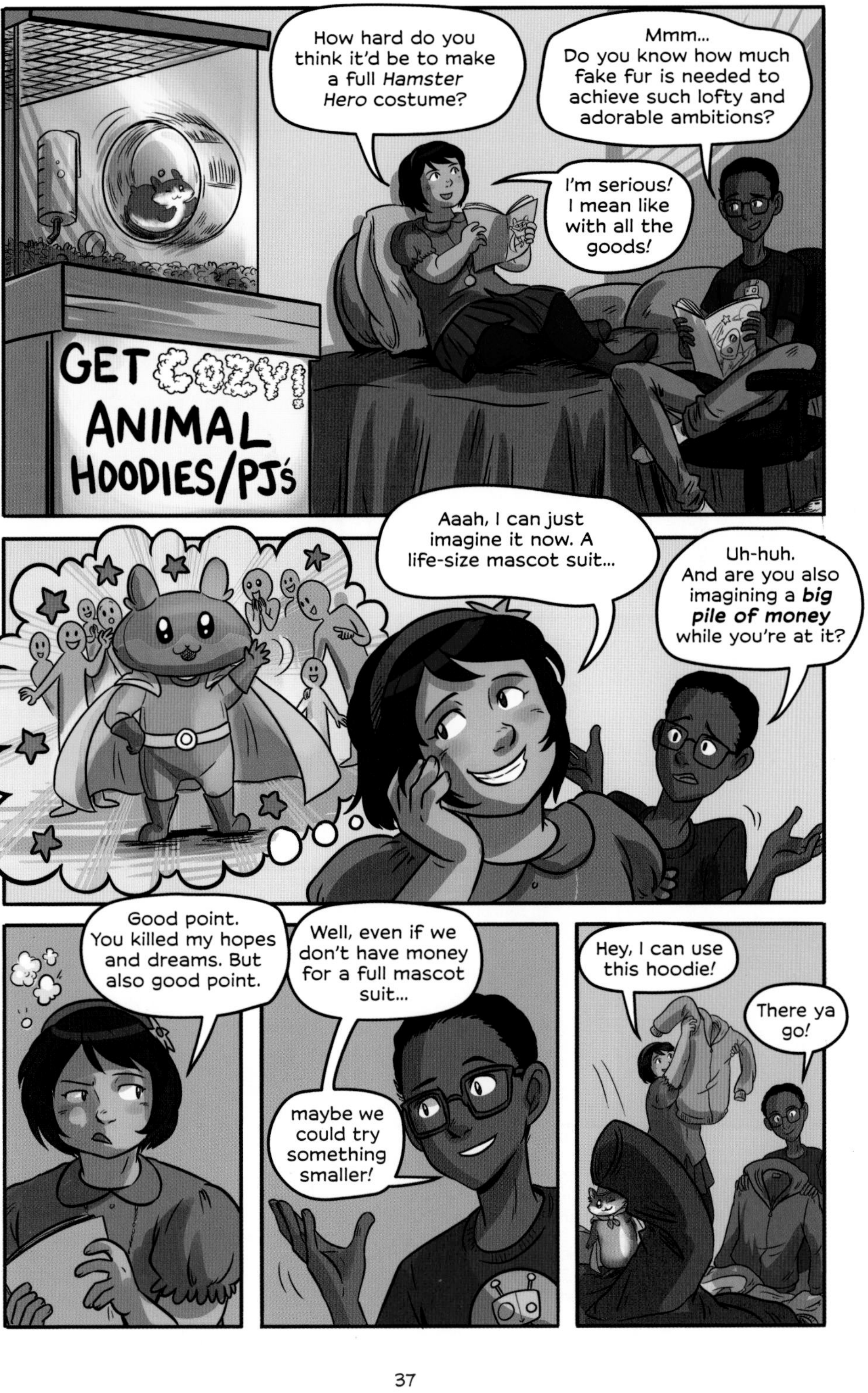
How hard do you think it'd be to make a full *Hamster Hero* costume?
Mmm... Do you know how much fake fur is needed to achieve such lofty and adorable ambitions?
I'm serious! I mean like with all the goods!
GET COZY! ANIMAL HOODIES/PJ's
Aaah, I can just imagine it now. A life-size mascot suit...
Uh-huh. And are you also imagining a ***big pile of money*** while you're at it?
Good point. You killed my hopes and dreams. But also good point.
Well, even if we don't have money for a full mascot suit...
maybe we could try something smaller!
Hey, I can use this hoodie!
There ya go!

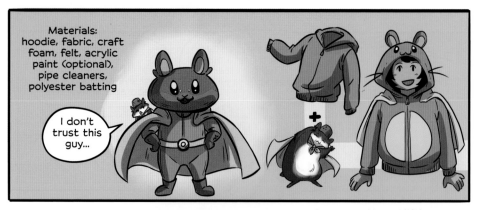

Materials: hoodie, fabric, craft foam, felt, acrylic paint (optional), pipe cleaners, polyester batting

I don't trust this guy...

Draw your ear shapes on the craft foam. Use your hoodie for size reference.

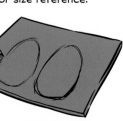

Cut out the pieces.

Trace a pattern 1/2" larger on the wrong side of your fabric.

Cut out four pieces from the fabric.

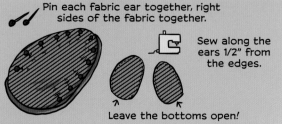

So you'll have:

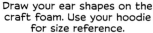

foam x 2

fabric or felt x 4

Pin each fabric ear together, right sides of the fabric together.

Sew along the ears 1/2" from the edges.

Leave the bottoms open!

Your fabric ears have an opening at the bottom.

Turn them right side out.

Insert a foam piece into each fabric ear.

The foam inserted into the ears will help your ears stand up!

Now sew along the bottom of each ear on the dotted line.

The idea is to trap the craft foam ear inside the fabric ear with the seam. Go slowly with your sewing machine so you can sew through the fabric and foam.

The ears are almost ready to be put on the hoodie!

You can also add accents to the ears in a different color, if you'd like.

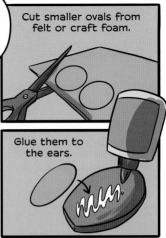

Cut smaller ovals from felt or craft foam.

Glue them to the ears.

You could also try fake fur!

Try on the hoodie, marking with chalk where the ears will sit on the hood.

Chalk lines!

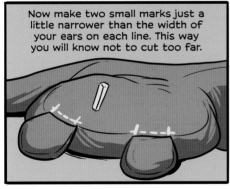

Now make two small marks just a little narrower than the width of your ears on each line. This way you will know not to cut too far.

Fold the fabric perpendicular to your lines.

SNIP!

And make a small cut along the chalk line.

Now lay the hood flat and cut along the chalk line, stopping 1/4" inside the little marks you made to show the width of each ear. Repeat for the other side.

SHARPEST

You'll get a cleaner cut with the part of the blade closest to the handle of the scissors.

Now push the ears into the incisions you've made. The ears should just barely squeeze through the opening.

Pin the ears in place in the front and back.

Cross-sectional view!

At least 1/2" of the ears should be inside the hoodie.

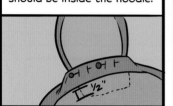

Thread your hand-sewing needle!

double knot

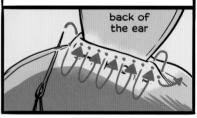

By hand sewing, you can sew through all of the layers easily. It would jam in the sewing machine.

You'll hand sew the ears to the hoodie.

Side view: needle and thread path per stitch.

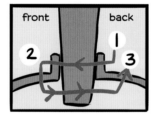

front     back

2     1     3

Here is the path of the needle. Start and finish sewing on the back of the ear.

back of the ear

Your stitching should extend about 1" on either side of each ear, so that there are no holes in the hood left next to the ears.

Think of it like the needle is jumping through three hurdles...

Over and over again, until the race is over.

Ugh... I'm glad I'm a hamster and not a *needle*...

ear

hoodie

hoodie

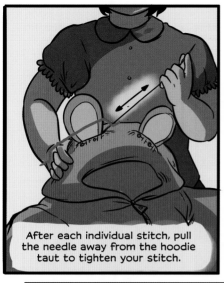

After each individual stitch, pull the needle away from the hoodie taut to tighten your stitch.

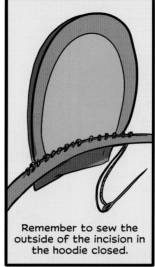

Remember to sew the outside of the incision in the hoodie closed.

When you've finished with an ear...

...double knot and cut the thread.

Now try on your hoodie again. Look at those perky ears!

This method can be applied to any ears you can think of!

Even a shark fin!

Hey, you went with the blue hoodie?

Yep! You like my fin?

Making Ears Review!

1. Cut craft foam pieces x 2.
2. Cut fabric pieces x 4.
3. Sew fabric ear pieces.
4. Turn fabric ears right side out.
5. Insert craft foam pieces.
6. Sew ears closed.
7. Add accents (optional).
8. Mark ear placement on hoodie with chalk.
9. Cut small incisions on hoodie and push ears inside incisions.
10. Pin ears in place.
11. Hand stitch ears to hoodie.
12. Knot and cut thread when finished stitching each ear.

Let's give your costume a face!

Cut eyes and a mouth out of craft foam or felt.

Glue in place.

For a shark, add black pupils to white or yellow!

Layer them in this order.

Don't forget gills!

You can also add highlights to the eyes.

white felt or craft foam

black (or whatever color you choose for the eyes) felt or craft foam

If you have more detailed eyes in mind, you can make your own eyes using the patch-making method from page 34!

To add whiskers, you'll need two pipe cleaners.

These are cheap and bend easily. They also come in a variety of colors.

Poke the end through.*

Bend the pipe cleaner inside the hood and push it through another hole.*

*Use a seam ripper to make the holes, if needed.

Tie a simple knot on the outside of the hoodie and pull it taut.

This keeps the whiskers in place!

knot

Give the shark some teeth!

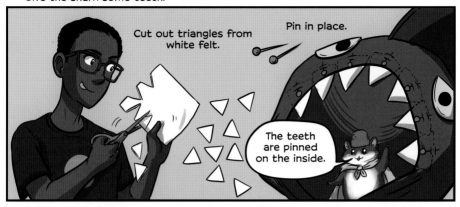

Cut out triangles from white felt.

Pin in place.

The teeth are pinned on the inside.

Sew the teeth in place all the way around the edge of the hoodie.

If you use the sewing machine, go slowly to accommodate all the layers of fabric.

Making the teeth out of felt ensures that they are easy on the eyes...

Your eyes, that is.

Optional: Adding a belly color!

Draw the shape of the belly markings you want on tracing paper. This is your pattern.

Cut the pattern out and use it to cut fabric in the color of your choice. Polar fleece is a good option for this!

Pin and sew each half of the belly in place on the front of your hoodie. Make sure the fabric is not puckered or wrinkled as you sew!

Keep your stitches 1/2" away from your zipper!

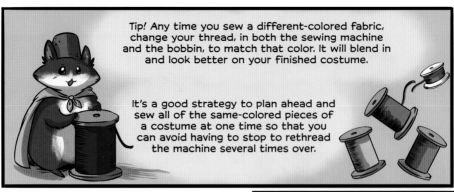

Tip! Any time you sew a different-colored fabric, change your thread, in both the sewing machine and the bobbin, to match that color. It will blend in and look better on your finished costume.

It's a good strategy to plan ahead and sew all of the same-colored pieces of a costume at one time so that you can avoid having to stop to rethread the machine several times over.

Now let's make a cape!
Fold a piece of fabric in half, with the right side of the fabric inside. Mark the pattern of the cape on the fabric with chalk.

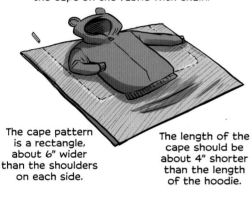

The cape pattern is a rectangle, about 6" wider than the shoulders on each side.

The length of the cape should be about 4" shorter than the length of the hoodie.

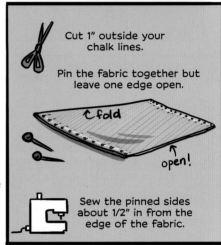

Cut 1" outside your chalk lines.

Pin the fabric together but leave one edge open.

↰ fold

open!

Sew the pinned sides about 1/2" in from the edge of the fabric.

The open end will be the bottom of the cape.

fold ↑

open ↓

Turn the cape right side out. Push the corners out gently.

Iron and press.

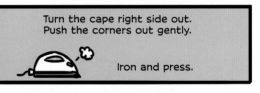

On the open edge: Fold the edges in about 1" and press with the iron.

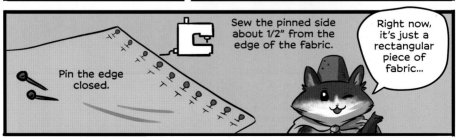

Pin the edge closed.

Sew the pinned side about 1/2" from the edge of the fabric.

Right now, it's just a rectangular piece of fabric...

Pin the top corners of your cape to the hoodie over the shoulders. The pins should be facing inward toward the hood, about 3" from the corners.

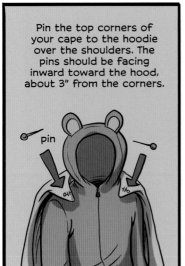

pin

Cut two 4" strips of sew-on Velcro for each shoulder.

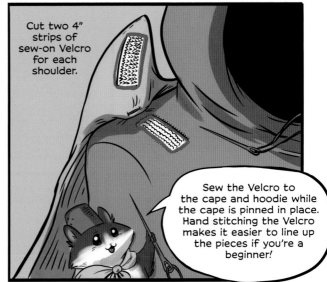

Sew the Velcro to the cape and hoodie while the cape is pinned in place. Hand stitching the Velcro makes it easier to line up the pieces if you're a beginner!

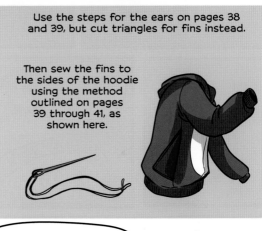

You can also add fins to the sides of the shark hoodie!

Use the steps for the ears on pages 38 and 39, but cut triangles for fins instead.

Then sew the fins to the sides of the hoodie using the method outlined on pages 39 through 41, as shown here.

Using these basic methods, you can add whatever decorative accents strike your fancy!

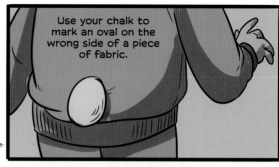

Use your chalk to mark an oval on the wrong side of a piece of fabric.

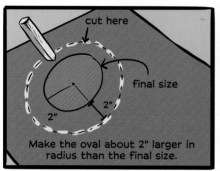

cut here

final size

2"

2"

2"

Make the oval about 2" larger in radius than the final size.

Cut two ovals from the fabric along the chalk line.

Pin the ovals together and leave a gap about 2" wide. You will stuff the tail through this opening later!

2"

Sew 1/4" from the edges, but leave the gap open!

Turn the tail right side out.

Now for some polyester batting!

Stuff the tail with the batting.

Don't put too much batting in the tail!

If it's overstuffed, the seams might burst!

Just right.

Aah! It's gonna blow!

Pull tight!

Hand stitch the tail closed.

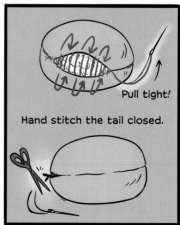

Now let's attach the tail to the hoodie!

The tail is going to be sewn to the hoodie here.

Make a small mark on the back of the hoodie with chalk for your reference.

Carefully hand stitch the tail flat against the hoodie.

Where the tail lies flush against the hoodie.

This can be a bit tricky because the tail is thicker and rounded. Securely hold the tail against the hoodie with one hand while you work.

Pay attention to where your needle is while you work.

You want to avoid sewing deeply into the tail, because the needle can get lost! Consider this area the *No Needle Zone*.

NO NEEDLE ZONE!

enter point
exit point

Your needle should go in and out with one stroke.

Tail →

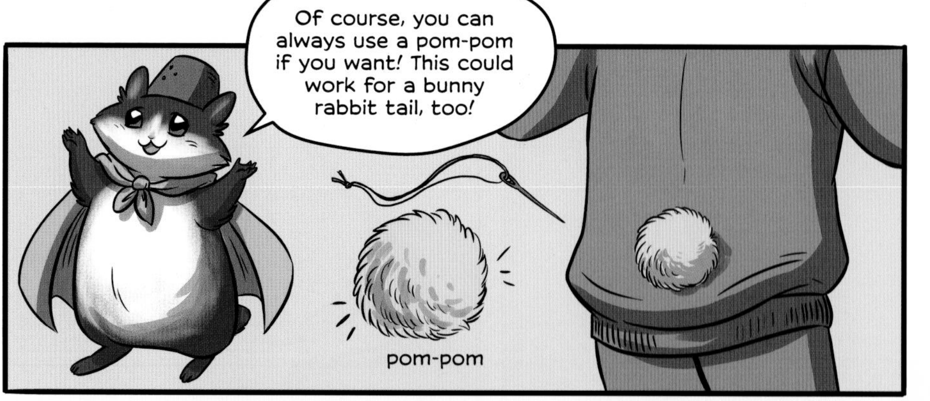
Of course, you can always use a pom-pom if you want! This could work for a bunny rabbit tail, too!
pom-pom

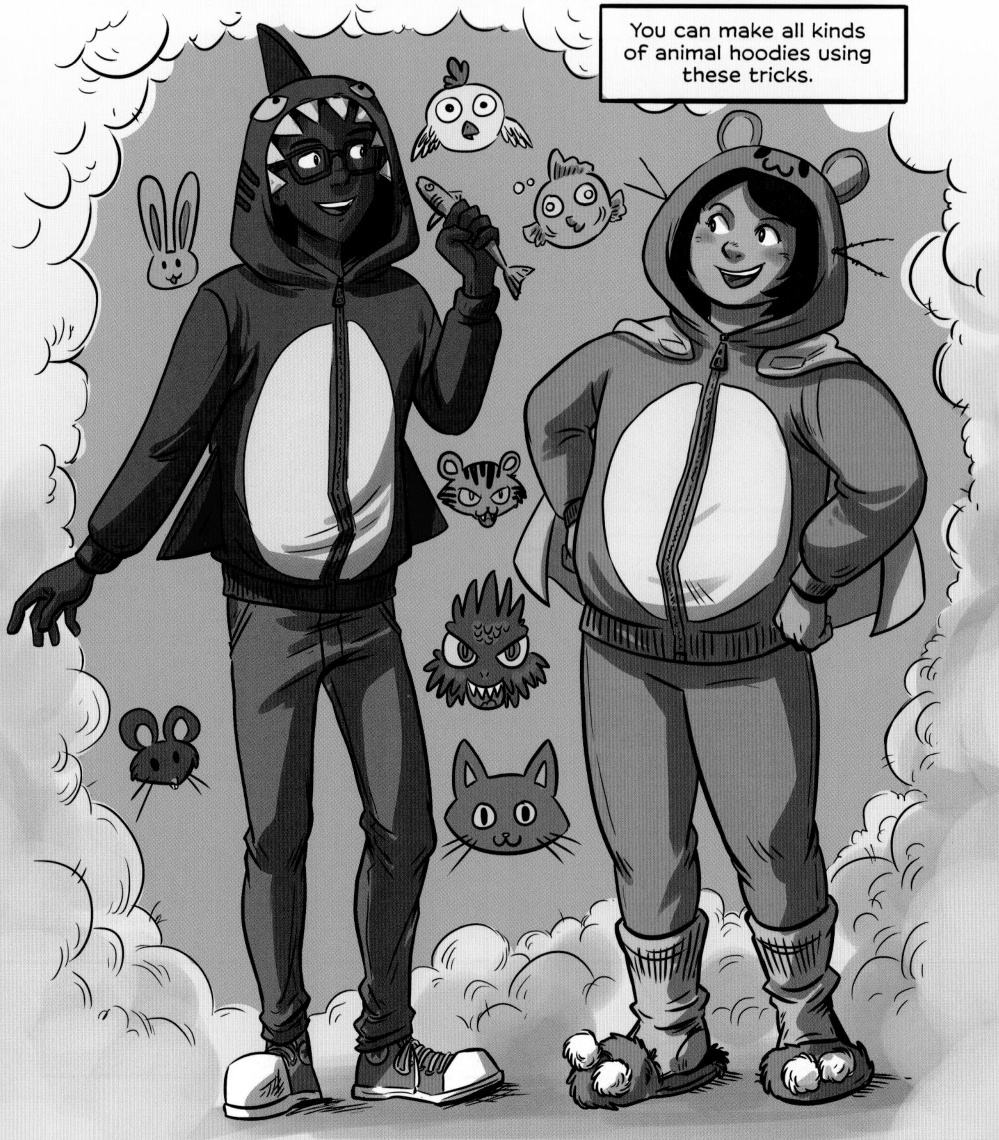
You can make all kinds of animal hoodies using these tricks.

How do you think they get all that leather out there in space? Like...every space outlaw is decked out in leather.

It just looks cool, I guess. Or maybe it's synthetic "space" pleather. I'm sure it's explained *rationally* somehow.

I'd rather go into outer space on a *real mission* with NASA.

*Pfft!* Not me, I'm *all about* sci-fi. Gimme some alien planets to explore!

# EXPLORE! SPACE TRAVELER ASTRONAUT

Yeehaww! See you, space cowpeeps.

There are a lot of different variations of space travelers found in science fiction these days—many of which look more like futuristic cowboys or characters found in the Wild West than actual astronauts who study in space.

Other sci-fi stories feature more realistic space suits, like those used by NASA.

Don't make me shoot first!

Depending on your resources, you could easily put together a space traveler outfit from plain old clothes and add your own insignias, accessories, and props. Or you can make a paper-mache helmet.

We'll discuss both approaches in this section of the book.

A parsec is a unit of LEEEEENGTH!

Space Traveler Materials:

old or secondhand clothes, acrylic paint, fabric paint, white fabric, old sunglasses, colored plastic sheet, craft foam, Rub 'n Buff, electrical tape, hot glue, craft glue, craft gems, elastic, felt, tracing paper, masking tape, newspaper

Pew pew!

Old clothes box, don't let me down!

Dark blue pants!

Hit those secondhand or thrift stores for other pieces like shirts...

$5.00

...and old leather or faux-leather vests.

Spiffy.

Sci-fi characters often have insignias of various space federations or fighter teams on their costumes. Make your own patch using the acrylic paint and cut out method on page 34.

Hand sew the patch to the vest or shirt.

Use hot glue or fabric glue as a shortcut if the vest material is too thick to sew through.

Intense. But I'm just wondering where the dude gets his hair styled.

If your character has a belt, here is how you can make your own custom buckle.

Draw and cut your buckle shape from craft foam.

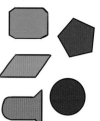

Yours might look different, depending on your character!

Here is a little trick to seal craft foam and make it nice and shiny! Use this whenever you need your foam to look like a metal or hard surface. I call this the glue, seal, and paint method.

1 part water

4 parts craft glue

Mix it up until it's smooth!

Make this in small batches, about 1/4 cup at a time!

plastic cup

Paint your craft foam buckle with the mixture, one side at a time. Let it seep into the foam.

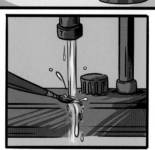

Rinse your brush right away so you can reuse it!

Let the first coat dry, and then paint it again. Repeat until the foam is glossy when dry.

The glue barrier will help keep the craft foam from absorbing the paint and looking dull.

Now you can paint the buckle with metallic silver or gold acrylic paint.

RUB N' BUFF

You can also use a product found in craft stores called Rub 'n Buff, which coats the item with metallic-colored wax.

Weather and add details to your buckle!

Now let's talk about something called **weathering**!

Weathering is when you purposefully alter the appearance of something to make it look worn down, damaged, or old.

Make sure your buckle is dry!

Dampen a paper towel...

Wring it out.

Squeeze a little black acrylic paint onto a paper plate.

Dip your paper towel in the paint and lightly dab the surface of the buckle; then spread the paint around and let it settle over the surface.

Back and forth!

Use a circular motion to get a more mottled effect!

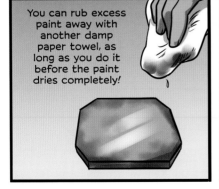

You can rub excess paint away with another damp paper towel, as long as you do it before the paint dries completely!

Add craft gems or shapes cut out of foam for buttons or other tech if you'd like!

craft glue

Now attach the buckle to the belt!

Measure around the fastened belt buckle and add an inch.

Cut a piece of elastic measuring that length.

Hot glue the ends of the elastic to the back of your buckle, making an elastic ring.

Cut and glue a piece of felt over the ends of the elastic to protect the ends.

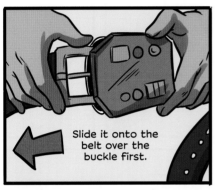

Slide it onto the belt over the buckle first.

Fasten the belt. Then slide your buckle back over on top of the original buckle.

Boom! A cheap and easy way to make a custom belt buckle!

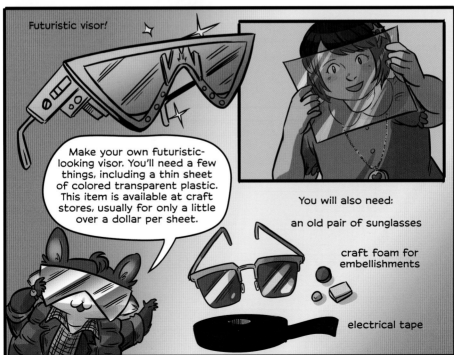

Futuristic visor!

Make your own futuristic-looking visor. You'll need a few things, including a thin sheet of colored transparent plastic. This item is available at craft stores, usually for only a little over a dollar per sheet.

You will also need:

an old pair of sunglasses

craft foam for embellishments

electrical tape

First, let's make a pattern for the visor!

On a sheet of paper, trace around a pair of old sunglasses.

Fold the paper in half.

This way, your pattern will be symmetrical.

Draw an interesting shape for your visor around the sunglasses outline!

Remember to leave a space for your nose!

Cut out your pattern.

This is the pattern you'll use to cut your plastic!

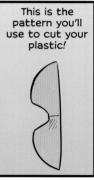

Lay your paper pattern on the colored plastic.

Trace the pattern and cut it out.

Don't use your fabric scissors for this!

Pop the lenses out of the sunglasses.

Now use a piece of electrical tape to fix the visor plastic to the top of the sunglasses frame.

Fold the tape over neatly and secure.

Ways to dress up your visor:

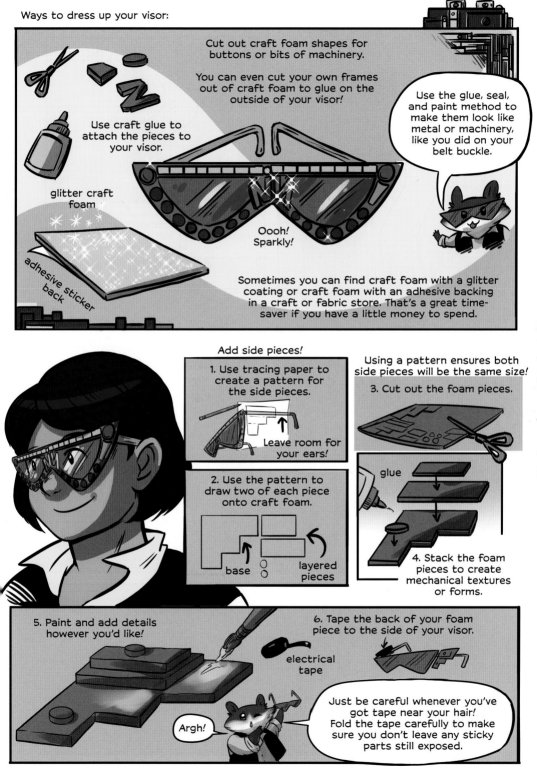

Cut out craft foam shapes for buttons or bits of machinery.

You can even cut your own frames out of craft foam to glue on the outside of your visor!

Use craft glue to attach the pieces to your visor.

Use the glue, seal, and paint method to make them look like metal or machinery, like you did on your belt buckle.

glitter craft foam

adhesive sticker back

Oooh! Sparkly!

Sometimes you can find craft foam with a glitter coating or craft foam with an adhesive backing in a craft or fabric store. That's a great time-saver if you have a little money to spend.

Add side pieces!

1. Use tracing paper to create a pattern for the side pieces.

Leave room for your ears!

2. Use the pattern to draw two of each piece onto craft foam.

base    layered pieces

Using a pattern ensures both side pieces will be the same size!

3. Cut out the foam pieces.

glue

4. Stack the foam pieces to create mechanical textures or forms.

5. Paint and add details however you'd like!

6. Tape the back of your foam piece to the side of your visor.

electrical tape

Argh!

Just be careful whenever you've got tape near your hair! Fold the tape carefully to make sure you don't leave any sticky parts still exposed.

Pair the vest, belt, buckle cover, and visor with a plain shirt underneath and plain dark pants.

Add craft foam accents to the vest!

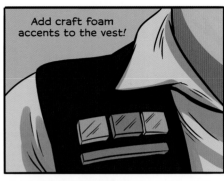

You can even modify a pair of plain pants to have a stripe up the side or add patches.

A quick way to do this is to use fabric paint to paint a stripe. Lay the pants flat and place folded newspaper inside the legs to keep the paint from leaking through.

Flip the pants so you are working on one leg at a time.

Use masking tape to keep your line straight when you paint.

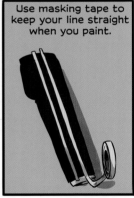

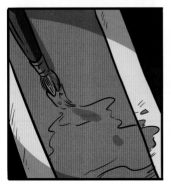

Paint one leg at a time and let the paint dry between layers—you may need to paint each stripe two or three times to get the paint to appear opaque on darker fabric.

Let it dry completely and then slowly and gently peel the masking tape off.

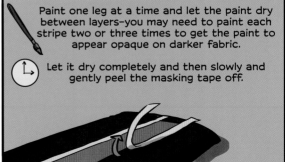

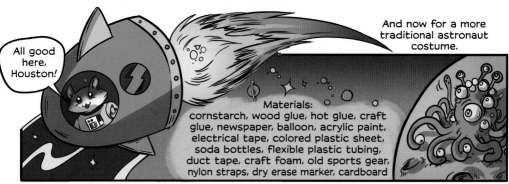

And now for a more traditional astronaut costume.

All good here, Houston!

Materials:
cornstarch, wood glue, hot glue, craft glue, newspaper, balloon, acrylic paint, electrical tape, colored plastic sheet, soda bottles, flexible plastic tubing, duct tape, craft foam, old sports gear, nylon straps, dry erase marker, cardboard

I'm pretty sure I can find a white shirt and sweat pants for this suit, but what about that helmet? Hmmm...

Baseball or football helmets? Naw, too heavy!

Hmm... Something lightweight... *Paper-mache!*

Cut newspaper into long strips about 3" wide.

Here's a recipe for super strong (but lightweight) paper-mache!

In a bowl, mix the following:
1/2 cup cornstarch
1/2 cup wood glue
1/2 cup water

Stir it until it's smooth!

Set up your work-station. This is going to be messy, so you'll need to put down some newspaper!

You're almost ready to start making your helmet.

Blow up a large balloon and tie the bottom.

Hold it up to your head. Make sure it is large enough for your head to fit within the space.

Is it tall enough?

Is it wide enough?

Dip a strip of newspaper into the paper-mache mixture and wet the entire strip.

Gently smooth the excess off.

Lay the strips on the balloon.

Build up a couple of layers, placing the paper in opposite directions.

Leave the bottom uncovered.

Let it dry completely.

KNOCK

Check to make sure it is completely dry!

Now pop the balloon!

POP!

58

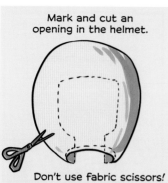
Mark and cut an opening in the helmet.

Don't use fabric scissors!

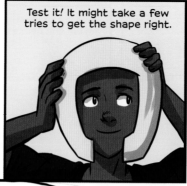
Test it! It might take a few tries to get the shape right.

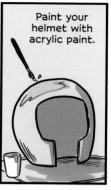
Paint your helmet with acrylic paint.

With household items like cardboard and empty soda bottles, you can make equipment for your astronaut costume.

You can find flexible tubing at a hardware store.

Tape two empty soda bottles together to make a jet pack.

duct tape

Sew the ends of a nylon strap together.

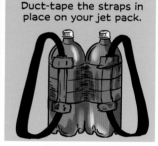
Duct-tape the straps in place on your jet pack.

Cover the pack with duct tape.

acrylic paint

You can also use cardboard pieces before you cover the pack with duct tape to alter the jet pack's shape and form!

Using the glue and seal method, create a panel of tech or machinery for your space suit! You can paint it white or metallic colors if you want!

CRAFT GLUE

Fix a length of tubing to the tops of the soda bottles with duct tape.

You can paint the tubing, too!

Optional: Use a transparent colored plastic sheet for a visor on your helmet!

For this project, blue or violet is a good choice, but it's up to you!

Insert the plastic inside the helmet, bending it to fit.

Mark around the edge of the helmet opening on the plastic with a dry erase marker.

Cut the visor shape out 2" larger than the outline. Then you can erase the marker.

Punch holes in the bottom to ensure good air circulation.

Tape the visor to the inside of the helmet with duct tape or electrical tape.

For the space suit itself, you can wear a white turtleneck. If you don't have this on hand, check thrift stores!

Use hot glue to attach the panel of "tech" to the front of your shirt.

Think about other items you may have in your closet that can be used for this costume!

What about winter gloves?

Or sweatpants?

And you can easily find boots at thrift stores for cheap.

Countdown! Adding those finishing touches!

You can also look at old sports equipment pieces for potential space suit gear.

When painted white with acrylic or spray paint, kneepads do the trick!

You may also want to secure your visor with hot glue on the lower edges.

Add decals or stickers on the sides of your helmet.

Now you're ready for anything outer space has in store!

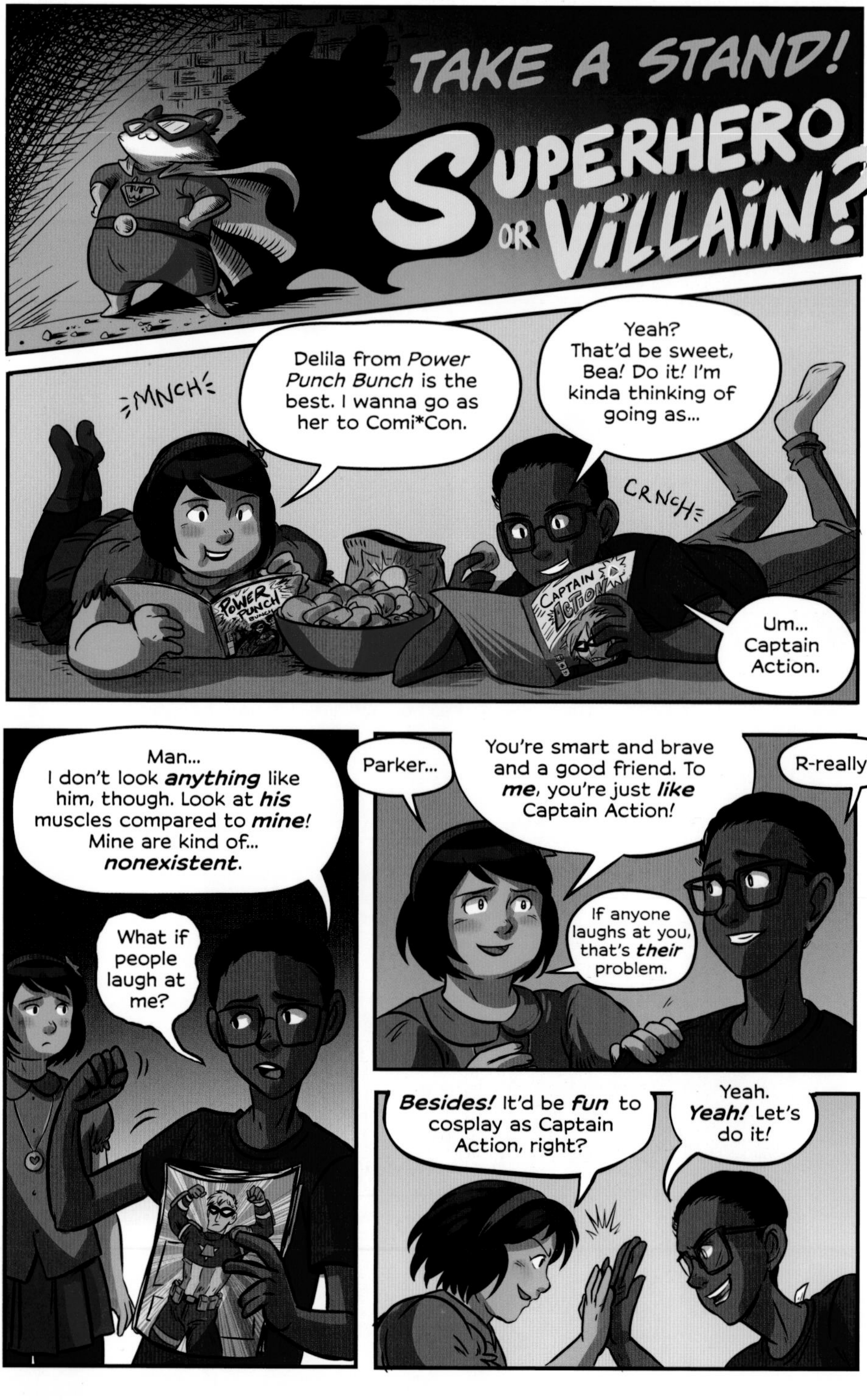

TAKE A STAND!
SUPERHERO OR VILLAIN?
MNCH
Delila from Power Punch Bunch is the best. I wanna go as her to Comi*Con.
Yeah? That'd be sweet, Bea! Do it! I'm kinda thinking of going as...
CRNCH
POWER PUNCH BUNCH
CAPTAIN ACTION
Um... Captain Action.
Man... I don't look anything like him, though. Look at his muscles compared to mine! Mine are kind of... nonexistent.
What if people laugh at me?
Parker...
You're smart and brave and a good friend. To me, you're just like Captain Action!
R-really?
If anyone laughs at you, that's their problem.
Besides! It'd be fun to cosplay as Captain Action, right?
Yeah. Yeah! Let's do it!

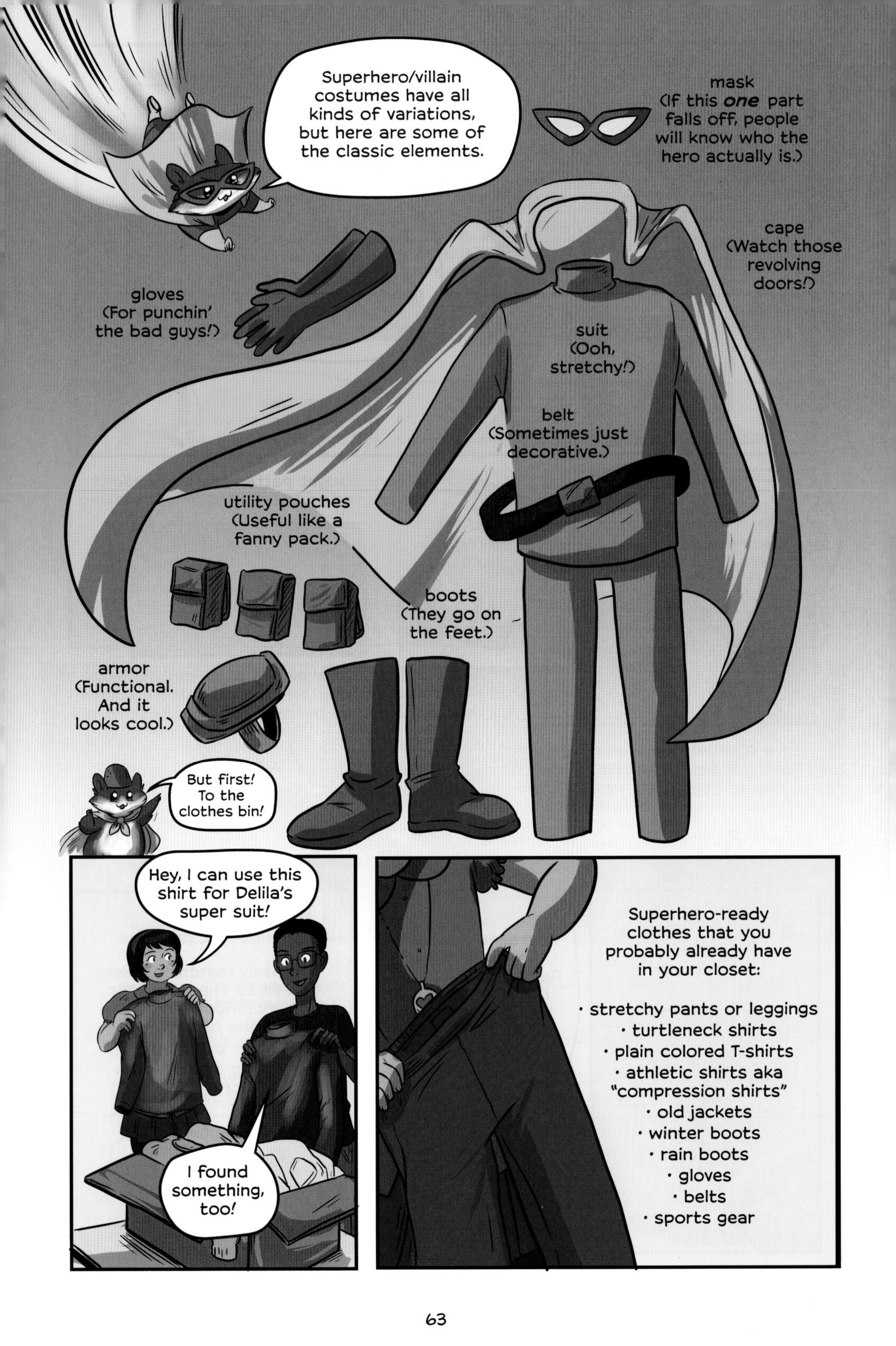
Superhero/villain costumes have all kinds of variations, but here are some of the classic elements.
mask
(If this *one* part falls off, people will know who the hero actually is.)
cape
(Watch those revolving doors!)
gloves
(For punchin' the bad guys!)
suit
(Ooh, stretchy!)
belt
(Sometimes just decorative.)
utility pouches
(Useful like a fanny pack.)
boots
(They go on the feet.)
armor
(Functional. And it looks cool.)
But first! To the clothes bin!
Hey, I can use this shirt for Delila's super suit!
I found something, too!
Superhero-ready clothes that you probably already have in your closet:
• stretchy pants or leggings
• turtleneck shirts
• plain colored T-shirts
• athletic shirts aka "compression shirts"
• old jackets
• winter boots
• rain boots
• gloves
• belts
• sports gear

Now you've got your cape...what about your super emblem?

One option is good old craft foam for a 3-D effect.

And of course, the patch painting method from page 34.

craft foam

acrylic painted fabric

These methods are useful in many ways. But what if you've got an emblem that needs to be *really* clean or precise?

If you've got a color printer and design software, you can make and print a design on iron-on transfer paper, and then put it on your suit!

IRON-ON TRANSFER PAPER FOR DARK FABRIC

You can buy this iron-on paper in craft or office supply stores.

Design the emblem on your computer.

CLICK

CLICK

Ooh, I just love it when my dreams come to fruition!

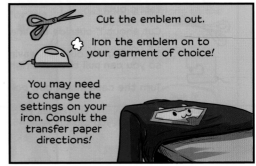

Cut the emblem out.

Iron the emblem on to your garment of choice!

You may need to change the settings on your iron. Consult the transfer paper directions!

Make your own stencil for a symbol!

Painting and adding details yourself is one of the fun parts of making costumes! But sometimes, even a great painter or artist needs a little guidance.

Look in craft stores for plain white sticker paper! This will be your stencil.

The advantage to using sticker paper is that you can stick it to the garment while you paint, keeping paint from smearing!

Draw your design on the sticker paper.

You'll need to cut the design out of the center. For this you need to use a craft knife or X-Acto blade.

X-Acto blades are useful for this because you can cut out isolated shapes from the paper.

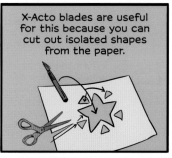

Carefully cut out the design with the blade.

It's ready to use!

To use the stencil, gently peel it from the backing.

Slooowly.

Stick the stencil to your shirt.

Apply fabric paint and let it dry.

It might take multiple coats of paint to get the color to stand out.

Let it dry completely before you gently peel the stencil off. Ta-daa!

A similar technique can be used to paint stripes.

Use masking tape to guide your lines as you paint– a little like that stencil.

For a character who's got stripes, this is a simple method!

Lay the tape down on your garment to guide you and paint away!

Let it dry completely, then gently pull the masking tape away.

Slooowly...

If your stripes alternate between two colors, completely finish painting one color and let it dry. Then tape your guides for the second color.

Apply the tape over the edge of the previous color so the stripes are flush.

Those are some straight stripes!

Another technique you can try is appliqué, which is the attachment of smaller pieces of fabric to a larger piece for decorative purposes.

3. Pin two pieces together for each stripe, right sides of the fabric together.

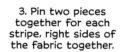

4. Sew each stripe together 1/2" from the edges, but leave one end open.

5. Turn the stripes right side out. Iron.

1. Lay tracing paper over your garment and mark the shape of your stripes on the paper.

6. Press the unsewn edge in with the iron and pin. Look at the wizard robe sleeves (page 33) for reference.

2. Use the pattern to cut two strips of fabric for each stripe, adding a 1/2" seam allowance around each stripe.

7. Sew the pinned end closed.

Now pin each stripe to the front of the garment, being careful not to pinch or wrinkle the fabric.

Carefully sew the stripes to the shirt. Gently stretch your shirt around the bed of the sewing machine so you don't sew through both sides!

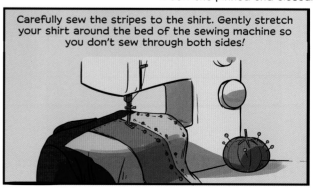

Crafting your shield!

First, make a circular pattern from a large piece of newspaper–about 2 feet in diameter. Make sure your pattern is about 1-2" larger than you'd like the shield, since you will trim the edges later. Divide it into twelve equally sized wedges. Refer to the witch hat project for help with drawing a circle pattern. Then trace your wedges onto the cardboard and cut them out with scissors or a craft knife.

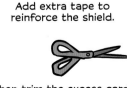

The grain/corrugation in the cardboard should run horizontally across each of your wedges for easier creasing in the next step.

Be careful with those blades!

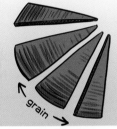
grain

To create the beveled form of the shield, you'll need to lightly crease the cardboard wedges at two or three points outward from the center of the disc. Crease each wedge at the same point to create a smooth curve to the entire shield.

cross section of a creased wedge

crease

crease

center of shield

crease

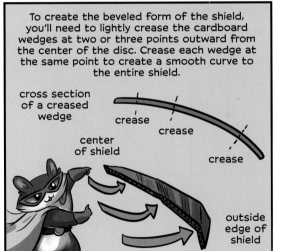

outside edge of shield

Once you have creased all of your wedges, use masking tape to fix them together, like so.

Press the shield down gently to even out the curve.

Add extra tape to reinforce the shield.

Then trim the excess cardboard off the edges so they are tidy!

Once you've finished trimming your shield and it's nice and round...

...reinforce the edge and the center even further with duct tape.

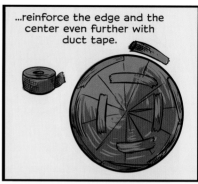

Duct tape is durable, has a strong grip, and it's waterproof.

It's stronger than masking tape because of all the little threads running through it!

Cover the rest of your shield with duct tape as evenly as possible.

Fold the tape over the outer edges about 2".

Make a grip for your shield out of craft foam. Cut a strip that measures the diameter of your shield in length and 3" wide.

Reinforce the craft foam by covering it with duct tape, on both sides!

Feel that power.

Now attach the strip to the back of the shield with hot glue under the ends. Leave a large enough gap for your arm to fit through! Then secure the ends of the strip with duct tape.

At this point, you can paint or decorate the shield however you like. (In this case, like Captain Action's shield!) If you want a smoother finish, spray the shield with some Plasti Dip before you paint it.

You can use spray paint, too.

Now, you'll tape your box together. First, the side/bottom panel will be taped to the back standing vertically; then the front goes on top!

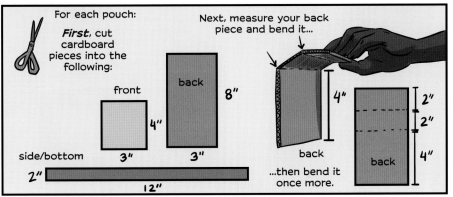

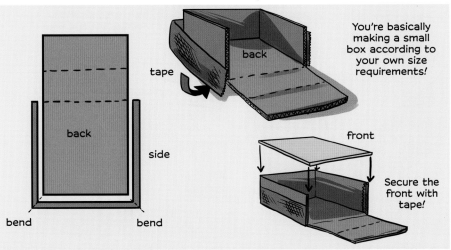

Cheerio! I'm **Bendy Cardboardpatch**. I'm here to inspect the pouches closely for gaps. If I find any, it means you'll need more duct tape in those areas to secure it.

Mind these gap-prone areas!

BOTTOM

Look inside, too.

If there are gaps in the bottom, you could lose the items you put inside the pouch!

And of course, you'll want to reinforce any dodgy or weakened areas with tape. Don't want the top of the pouch breaking off during the convention!

Can someone let me out?

Once you're happy with your pouch's construction, you can paint the pouch any color you want. Brown acrylic paint in combination with the weathering method from page 52 works great for making it look like leather!

Next, you'll want to add Velcro so you can open and close your pouch. Stick some Velcro to the inside of the top with hot glue.

Velcro

Do the same on the front where the top meets it when closed.

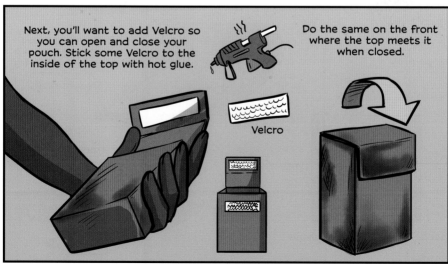

Attach the pouches to the belt!

For each pouch, tear a strip of duct tape at least 4" long.

4"

Fold the tape in half lengthwise to make a super strong strap.

This strap will go on the back of each pouch.

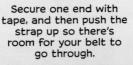

Secure one end with tape, and then push the strap up so there's room for your belt to go through.

Add a strap to all of your pouches.

Slide your pouches on to the belt so they are facing outward.

Fasten your belt and pull the pouches around the sides.

Using the belt buckle cover method found on pages 51-53, you can make a buckle to finish the look!

elastic

hot glue

craft foam

acrylic paint

Rub 'n Buff for a metallic sheen

Slide your belt buckle cover on!

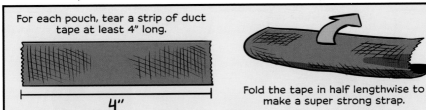

Howdy, Captain Action! How's it going?

Not bad! I've still gotta make his *armor* pieces, though...

Armor, huh? Isn't his made of some kind of Super Neptonian Metal Alloy in the original comic run from 1934?!

Huh?

*Whoa*, is it? You've got an awesome memory. Mine'll have to be made with what we have here...but I'm not worried.

Besides fabric, these are some of the other materials you've used...

cardboard

masking tape

fabric and acrylic paints

Rub 'n Buff

craft foam

duct tape

Plasti Dip sealant

craft and fabric glue

hot glue

felt

CRAFT GLUE

FABRIC GLUE

PLASTI-DIP

You've got this!

Yeah, I'll figure out a way!

When tackling something like armor, don't panic. It's all about problem-solving.

First, look at your source material. Study it carefully.

Sometimes, even after an internet search, it's difficult to find a schematic or straight-on image of a character's costume for reference, or the images may be inconsistent.
So you can:
1. *Analyze* the shapes you see.
2. *Simplify* those shapes.
3. *Draw* the design again.

shoulder

gauntlet

Make a mock-up (test) pattern out of paper.

Hmm. A bit too wide.

If it's too wide, give it a trim!

*This is a process called trial and error!*

Keep trying until you get the right shape and size for your pattern! You'll learn what works by trying it.

*Shoulder Pattern!* You're accused of being cut too wide at the top. How do you plead?

Guilty, Your Honor.

Once you're satisfied with your mock-up pattern, you can start producing the armor pieces!

In this particular instance, you may want to work with cardboard.

grain/corrugation

Trace your pattern pieces on the cardboard. Consider the direction of the corrugation with regard to where you will need to bend or fold the armor pieces.

It's much easier to bend cardboard parallel to the corrugation grooves.

You may not always choose cardboard for a project. There's also foam and other materials to consider.

Because you are most familiar with cardboard and craft foam at this point, let's compare those two materials.

Cardboard
· Durable and lightweight
· Cheap (Use up those old boxes!)
· Harder to achieve a smoother edge or surface
· Bends in mostly straight angles along corrugation (can be limiting)

Craft Foam

· Flexible and lightweight (extremely so!)
· Cheap
· Not very durable unless prepared with a sealant such as glue or Plasti Dip and/or reinforced with a fabric backing

Cardboard Finishing Methods

· Reinforce with duct tape or masking tape.

· Combine with paper-mache to strengthen.

· Coat with craft glue before painting to achieve a glossier finish.

OR

· Coat with Plasti Dip (optional).

· Apply acrylic paint.

Craft Foam Finishing Methods

· Use the glue and seal method from page 51.

· Reinforce with fabric applied with glue, like the witch or wizard hat on pages 30-33. (Increases durability, but not to cardboard levels!)

· Coat with Plasti-Dip (optional).

· Apply acrylic paint.

When you've cut your cardboard pieces, you can add ridges to them by gluing narrow pieces of cardboard or craft foam to the base, and then paint them.

To wear it, you'll need to attach elastic to the armor.

Leave yourself an extra 2-3" so the elastic isn't too tight!

Hot glue the elastic to the inside of the armor.

Velcro

Reinforce the bond with duct tape. For some pieces, like the shoulder pads, you may want to add Velcro in addition to elastic.

To wear the armor, gently slide it on over your costume.

Tip! When you have multiple copies of a piece to make, like the pouches or armor, treat your work like an assembly line! Do one step for all the pieces and then move on to the next step.

What do you think?

Hey, awesome! See, you were worried for nothing.

Who is that *Masked Ham*?!

On a sheet of craft foam, draw half of your mask shape.

Remember to leave space for your nose!

Now fold the sheet in half.

Holding the craft foam sheet together, cut out the mask along the fold.

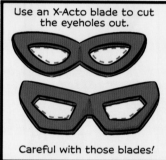

Use an X-Acto blade to cut the eyeholes out.

Careful with those blades!

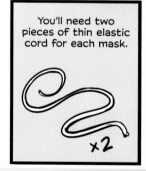

You'll need two pieces of thin elastic cord for each mask.

x2

Put a piece of masking tape on the outer corner of your mask to reinforce it (on the back).

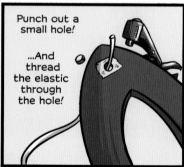

Punch out a small hole!

...And thread the elastic through the hole!

TA- DA!

Repeat on the other side of the mask, and make sure it fits comfortably before you tie the cords together in the back!

From here, you can paint your mask using the craft glue sealing method on page 51.

Tie the elastic looser if you'll be wearing your mask over glasses.

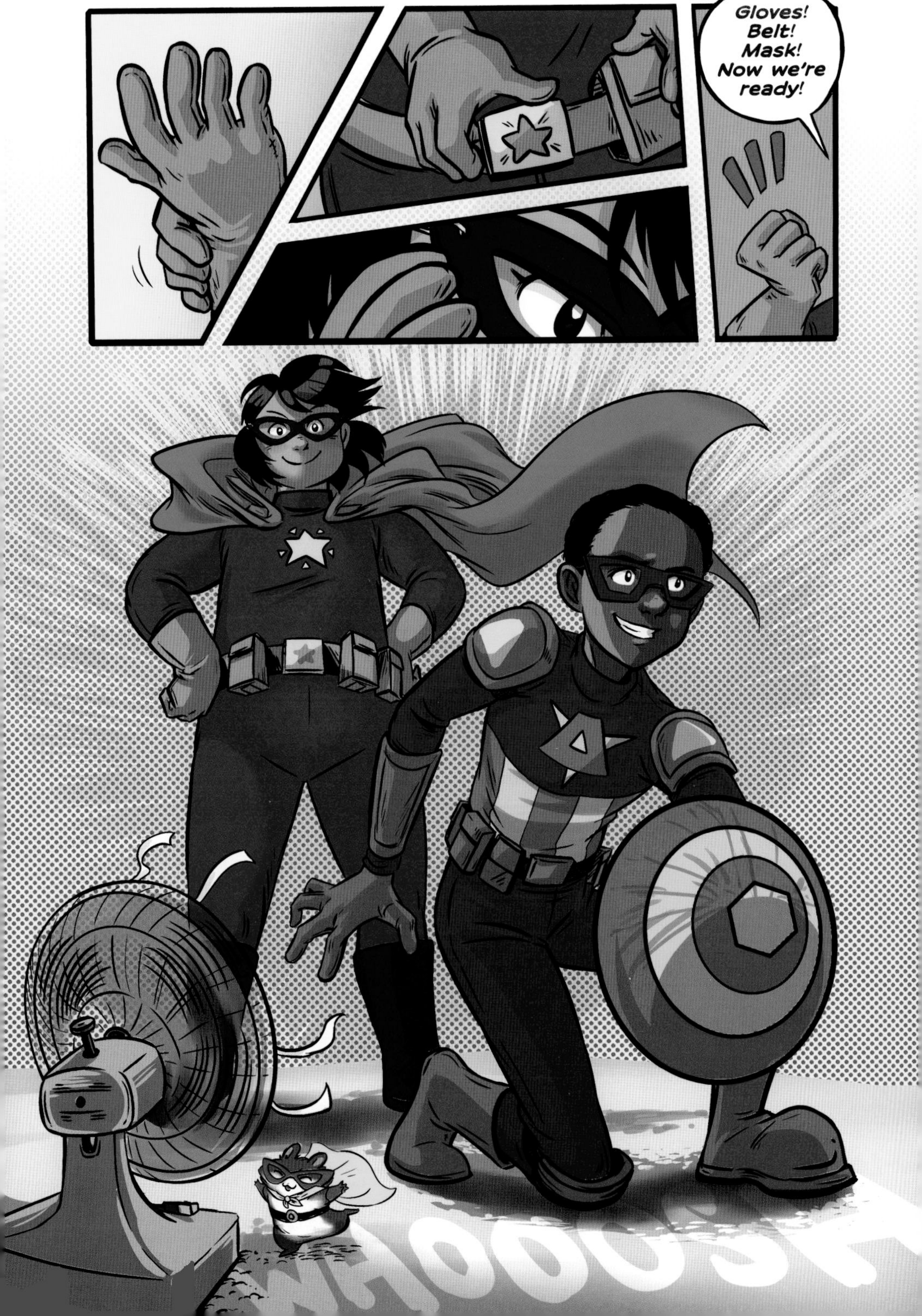
Gloves! Belt! Mask! Now we're ready!
WHOOOSH

So how're you feeling now?

Better! I mean, I think...

...but do you really think we'll **look** like the characters?

Hmmm...

Hrm...

KIRBY KAKES

POWER PUNCH

*Hmmmm.*

Hahaha, *nope!*

POWER PUNCH

Huh?

But they're drawings! Of course we won't look *just like them!*

It's fun to *pretend* to be them, though!

*The power's in the pose.*

I never thought of it that way.

Having fun is what costume making is all about.

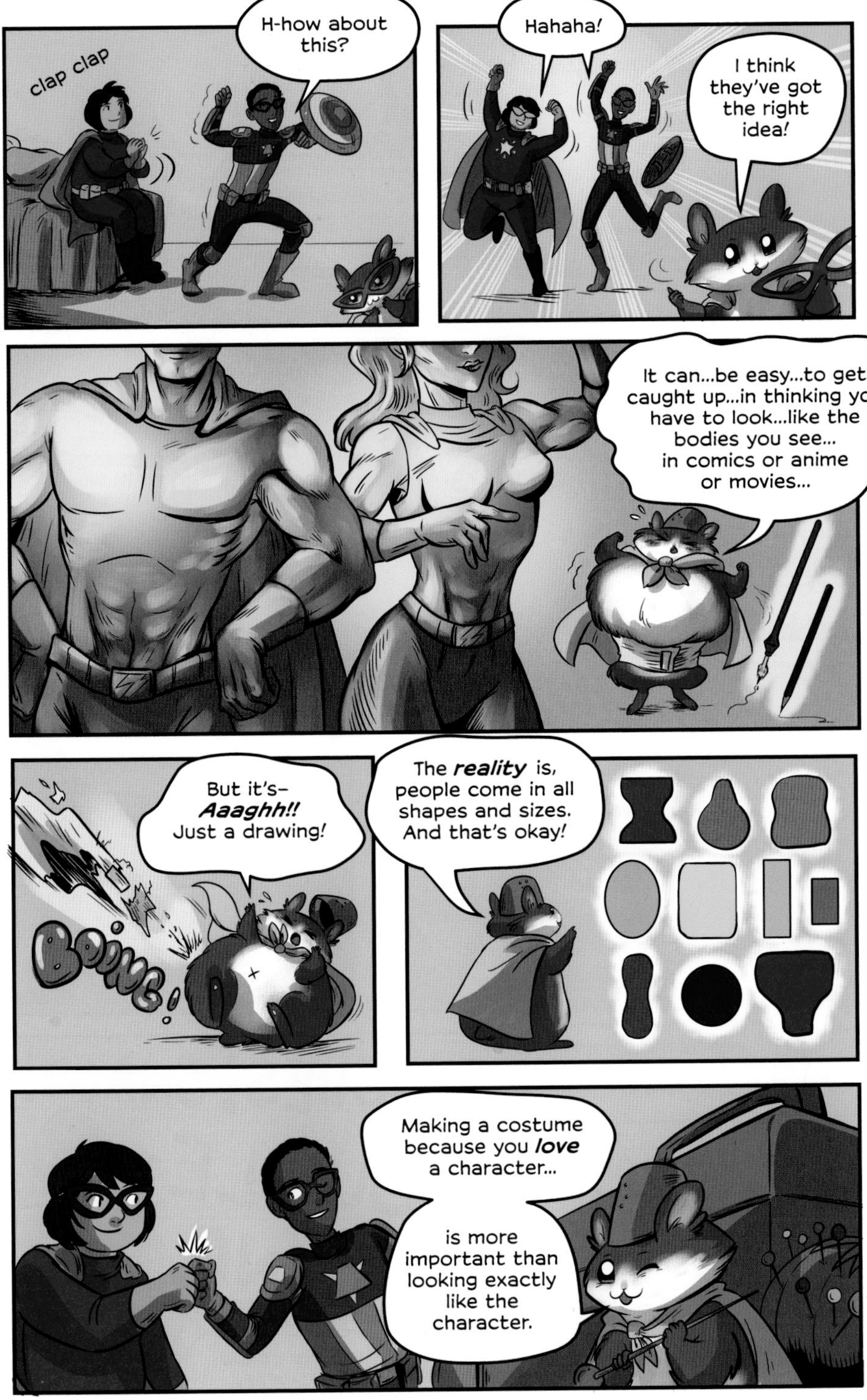
H-how about this?
clap clap
Hahaha!
I think they've got the right idea!
It can...be easy...to get caught up...in thinking you have to look...like the bodies you see... in comics or anime or movies...
But it's– *Aaaghh!!* Just a drawing!
BOING!
The *reality* is, people come in all shapes and sizes. And that's okay!
Making a costume because you *love* a character...
is more important than looking exactly like the character.

Sometimes, you have days where you're not so confident about your skills.

I'm kinda curious... how do you think our costumes will measure up at the con?

Yikes. Do I want to go down this rabbit hole? What happened to Miss Positive?

I'm just saying. It couldn't hurt to take a look...

tak tak tak

BOOGLE

COMICON COSPLAYERS

SEARCH   CLEAR

*Whoaah.*

AWESOMENESS

Uh, okay. Those are some *amazing* costumes...

I'm freaking out.

It's okay to be nervous before a convention. But don't let it get to you! We'll talk a little about soothing those first time jitters.

SUNFLOWER DIGEST

Man, I didn't realize there were **so many** top-tier cosplayers going...

E-ever feel like your stomach has a bunch of butterflies in it?

TANGLES! SNAGS! TROUBLE-SHOOTING

Let's get those butterflies under control!

82

The best defense against worry is *knowledge!* Look at the convention's website to start. Do this in advance so you know what to expect!

Oh! Hey, here's Comi*Con's website. Look, right here it has a page *just* about costumes and cosplay.

Hmm. Hey, it's got an anti-harrassment policy.

WELCOME TO COMI*CON
COSPLAY

Most conventions nowadays have anti-harrassment policies in place. This means that the con takes a hard stance against people behaving disrespectfully toward one another at the con.

It also helps to look at experienced convention goers' blogs for tips!

List of common Anime/Comic Convention Policies:
(These vary by convention, so always check with the con itself!)

· No harassment toward other con goers or guests will be tolerated.
· No realistic weapons or sharp-edged props allowed.
· Peace-bonding* is required for prop weapons.
· Generally, if it's illegal outside the con, it's illegal inside the con.

*Peace-bonding is a conspicuous lock, tie, or mark, which makes or identifies something as unusable and shows that the owner's intentions are purely peaceful.

It makes me feel better to know that the con is stating officially that they don't tolerate people being jerks.

Yeah.

Make your own con plan. Agree on what to do if you get separated, and exchange your emergency phone numbers and contact info.

BEA + Parker's AWESOME CONVENTION PLAN!

Emergency contact: Parker's Mom

Meeting place if we get separated: The fountain in front of the convention center.

Bea will carry an extra EpiPen for Parker.

Be awesome.

Convention web forums or blogs run by other fans who have more con-going experience can yield even more information, such as...

- How many people usually attend the convention

- If there are any issues related to crowding or an attendance cap

- Places to get food nearby

- Local restaurants and when to go to avoid waiting for a table or food

- Directions to the convention and local transportation tips

- Money-saving tips for budget planning

- General tips for first-time attendees

- Convention or area "quirks" to consider

Attend local comic or anime club meetings, too! You can meet fellow fans who might have con-going experience to share with you!

So, Emma, what was it like at last year's Comi*Con? Do you have any tips?

Oh. Em. Gee. *Yes*. It was the best three days of my *life*...

See? You're already rounding up those pesky butterflies just by doing some research!

You can get some great tips and suggestions from others with convention experience.

Looking at specific events on the convention page can help you plan what kinds of things you might want to take with you, just in case.

There's a good sushi place right next to the convention center!

But don't go to the BurgerMac on 45th Street. That place is *nasty*.

NOTES

Take notes!

Plan ahead! If you know you'll be in costume at a convention all day...

...pack clothes just in case you want to change or take a break from cosplaying.

Don't hesitate to take a backpack with you.

Cons are a lot of fun, but like all big events, you'll have more fun if you're *well prepared*!

It's a good idea to pack:

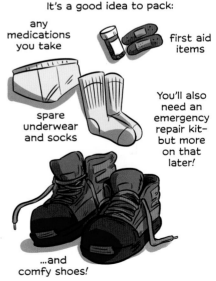

any medications you take

first aid items

spare underwear and socks

You'll also need an emergency repair kit– but more on that later!

...and comfy shoes!

It's okay if you're a little shy about cosplaying!

Practicing poses before the con can help build your confidence.

The pose you strike while in costume can express a lot about a character!

Are they *brave*? Shy? *Fierce*?! Sweet? Stoic? Cute?

Practicing poses before the convention also:

· Builds your confidence.

· Helps you feel more comfortable with your costume and can be a good way to test the fit and durability of your costume pieces.

· Is a good way to make sure you've got all your costume parts together before packing.

Practicing poses is like a dress rehearsal. But what if something goes wrong before showtime? Let's look at some possible snags that you might face and their fixes!

Oh!

Whoops!

What happened?

The seam in my sleeve ripped.

# HOW-TO: COSTUME REPAIR

Ready, Doctor?

Ready, Doctor!

The problem: A popped or ripped seam!

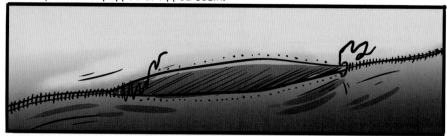

1. Turn the garment inside out and fold it in half along the seam.

2. Pin it closed.

ripped seam

3. Starting a few inches away from the rip, run the seam through the sewing machine again, closing the ripped seam. Finish a few inches away, too.

You can also hand stitch the ripped seam closed!

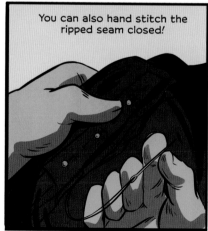

Trim the broken threads and tie your new stitches off neatly at the ends.

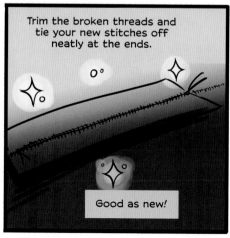

Good as new!

The problem: A snag in the sewing machine!

whrrrrrr

Aaah! The lovely sound of a sewing machine working smoothly.

CLANK!

No, no! Nononono!

Oh, great. A snag.

Take a deep breath, undo the snag, and rethread.

If you find yourself getting too frustrated, take a break and walk away from the project entirely for a bit.

Reread the instruction manual carefully. Each sewing machine is different, and manuals usually have a troubleshooting section.

TROUBLESHOOTING

Tangled thread in the lower portion of the sewing machine can take patience to fix. Don't be afraid to ask for help when you need it!

Going into the caverns of the sewing machine can be thirsty work, especially when there's a jam!

## Sewing Machine Troubleshooting *safety*!

· Always *unplug* the machine first!
· Never stick your fingers where there are moving parts.
· If the thread is tangled too deeply, ask for help!
· Do not poke sharp objects into the machine to try to dislodge the bobbin.
· Search online for troubleshooting videos

Cleaning up your work space before you try tackling any sewing machine or sewn fabric snags will make it much easier (and safer!) for you to troubleshoot.

Do the following if you find yourself getting frustrated...

lint roller

Use a lint roller to pick up stray threads that fall onto the floor or crowd the sewing machine.

Aaah, refreshing!

HAZARD!

You can't fix anything if you can't see what you're doing!

Make it a habit to clean up your work area often.

Fold your fabric and put everything in its proper place.

Now you can continue tackling problems without a messy work space distracting you.

FABRIC

OLD CLOTHES

The problem: Part of the costume is pulling, or the fabric is puckering when you wear it!

Huh. Must've missed that before!

1. Take a look at the seam holding the fabric together and make sure it is lying straight.

There's the problem!

The fabric may have gotten caught while you were sewing.

2. Sometimes you need to use your *seam ripper* to fix the seam if it is uneven or crooked.

The seam ripper is surprisingly *sharp*, so be careful!

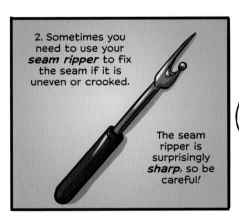

3. Carefully insert the seam ripper with the blade facing the stitches. Gently push it through the stitch.

Careful not to rip the fabric!

Here's the seam ripper in action, up close. The blade cuts the threads.

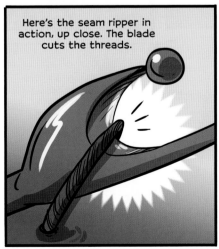

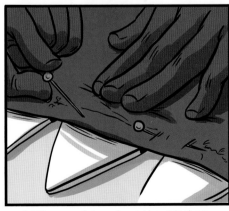

4. When you've undone the stitches, pin the fabric in place again.

Sometimes part of the fabric gets caught in the seam while you are sewing, and you don't notice it until after you are done. If that is the case, then you may need to take the stitches out and resew part or all of that seam again so it lays flat.

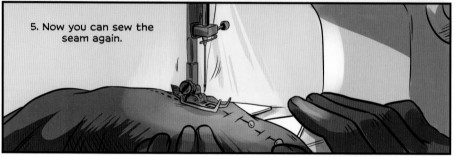

The problem: Parts of your costume chafe or hurt!

Ouch!

Armor looks cool, but it's not worth it if it's painful to wear! Here are ways you can make sure that it's comfortable and safe.

Ensure that the parts of the costume that are in contact with your skin don't have any exposed seams or pieces of material that could chafe or poke you. Glue felt backings to armor pieces that might come in contact with skin to make sure that the hard pieces don't rub during wear.

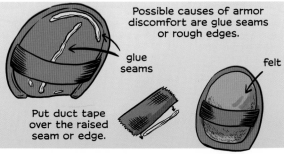

Possible causes of armor discomfort are glue seams or rough edges.

glue seams

felt

Put duct tape over the raised seam or edge.

Make sure the elastic isn't too tight!

Ouch.

Adding an extra inch or two to the elastic bands on your armor can make a *huge* difference in your comfort level.

This is why it's always a good idea to do a test run for your costume before you go to a convention!

You'll catch any problems early on and you'll have enough time to fix them.

Make sure you can sit, bend over, lean back, and walk comfortably while wearing the costume!

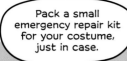

Pack a small emergency repair kit for your costume, just in case.

fabric glue

scissors

Pack it all in a plastic bag!

thread

FABRIC GLUE

Put a sewing needle through a piece of paper for safe travel.

sewing needle

duct tape

safety pins

Well, I'm feeling a *lot* better now. How about you, Bea?

Yeah, definitely! The excitement is setting in.

I recorded all the plans in my notebook! We are clear for liftoff.

Hey, uh... so, I was kind of thinking about trying one more costume... y'know...

Uh. Bea?

*Huhuhuhu...* You've read my mind.

*Count me in!*

WEIRD S.F.
S・F マガジン

So extra.

# SCARY! ALIEN OR MONSTER

Kinda like how Kaiju and monster designs almost always look like reptiles or lizards.

Some aliens resemble bugs. They're pretty cute, actually!

Honeybee

Bearded Dragon Lizard

## Alien Costume

Eyes. Lots of them.

antennae

bug-like fuzz

super retro-inspired space dress

flared skirt

## Monster Costume

Lizard-like scales. Lots of them.

protruding eyes

claws

teeth

Not a guy in a rubber suit, but close!

tail (optional)

Materials: old clothes, fabric, craft foam, felt, cardboard, acrylic paint, fabric paint, pom-poms, ping-pong balls

Look in secondhand stores for old dresses or garments if you don't have one already!

Add accents to an old dress to make it an alien space outfit. Use fluorescent or vibrant fabric paint against a dark dress.

Prep your workstation, as always, by putting down some newspaper.

You could also go with scales, instead!

Cut the scales from foam or felt and glue them in a layered pattern.

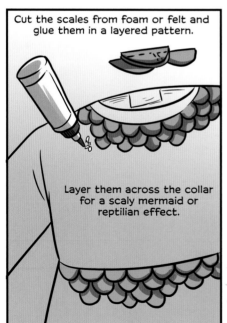

Layer them across the collar for a scaly mermaid or reptilian effect.

This costume doesn't have to be a dress! It can also be a T-shirt or a long-sleeved shirt!

Sharp geometric shapes make it look futuristic or otherworldly.

Remember the animal ears from pages 38-39?

Use that same technique to insert unusual shoulder forms into your costume.

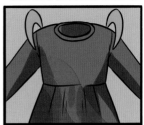

The forms are going into the shoulder seams!

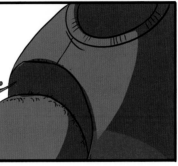

Once you've got your shoulder pieces cut from craft foam and covered in the fabric of your choice, remove the seams in the tops of the shoulders.

Don't remove the whole seam!

Pin the foam shapes in place.

Just like how you hand stitched the ears into the hoodie on pages 39-40, you'll do the same here with the shoulder pieces!

Hand stitch the foam pieces between the opened sleeve and dress shoulder hem.

The dotted line shows the foam shape inside the sleeve, about 1" down from the top of the shoulder hem.

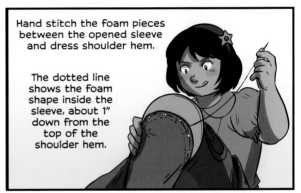

The needle will go through the sleeve, the foam, and the dress in each stitch.

Stitch 1" past the portion where you removed the seams to close any gaps.

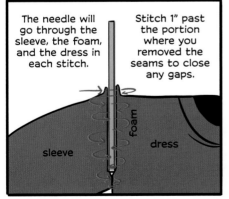

foam

sleeve          dress

This is a quick way to make your garment look alien.
And a little bit '70s, too.

Add a ring of fabric in an accent color to the bottom of the dress to give it a bit of flair...and flare!

The goal here is to get the bottom of the dress to flare outward.

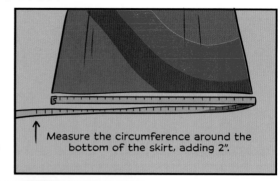

Measure the circumference around the bottom of the skirt, adding 2".

For this, you'll need some foam pipe insulation tubing. It's cheap at about $1.99 for six feet.

Cut foam tubing to your circumference measurement.

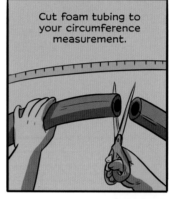

Cut a slit open along the full length of the tube.* This will help it roll smoothly.

Lay your tubing on a piece of fabric in the accent color of your choice. The fabric should be longer than the tube by about 4" and wide enough to cover the tube with 2-3" of seam allowance. Fold it over the tube tightly, pin in place, and cut the fabric, including 2-3" extra for seam allowance.

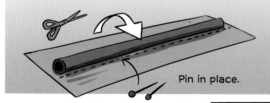

Pin in place.

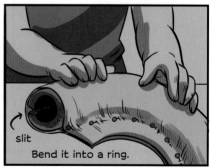

slit

Bend it into a ring.

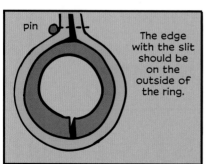

pin

The edge with the slit should be on the outside of the ring.

Pin the tube to the bottom of the dress 2" from the hem. The edge of the fabric covering the tube should point down toward the bottom hem of the dress.

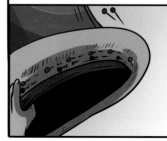

With the unfinished edges of the fabric underneath, hand stitch to the bottom hem of your dress.

*Some foam pipe insulation comes with a slit already cut in it.

Again, when sewing the tubing to the dress, make sure your seam is *under* the dress opening so it's not visible when you are finished.

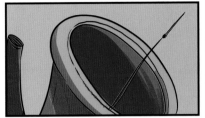

cross-sectional view

dress

fabric-covered tube

inside tube

seam

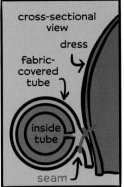

You're only sewing the fabric portion of the tube to the dress.

fabric-covered tube

bottom hem of dress

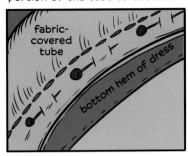

Sew the ends of the fabric covering the foam tube together in the back to close.

inside of the dress

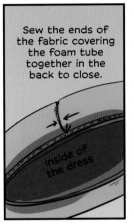

Now you've got a dress with a flared bottom hem that looks a little spacey when you move!

cross-sectional view

Here's what the bottom looks like when you're done!

Make an antennae headband with eyeballs!

headband

optional: craft-grade lightweight metal springs!

pipe cleaners

pom-poms

felt or craft foam shapes

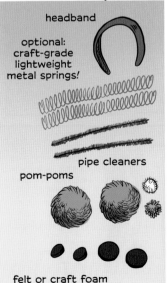

Curl the pipe cleaner around the top of the headband and twist it twice around the headband. Secure it with some hot glue. Twist the pipe cleaner around your finger a few times to make a coil.

hot glue

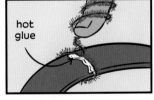

Glue pom-poms to the top and add felt shapes to create eyeballs.

Add as many as you want. There are no rules about how many eyes aliens have. Yet, anyway!

Another idea is to get a fuzzy craft boa and cut it to fit the headband, and glue that to the base of the headband before you add more eyeballs...

...to make it a fuzzy alien.

Absolutely. Terrifying.

Half-sphere clear acrylic ornaments sold in craft stores also make great costume pieces.

Here's how to make a sparkly alien headpiece using these.

Trace around the ornament half-spheres on a piece of cardboard.

This will be your base.

Cut the cardboard circles out about 1/4" larger than your mark.

Paint the cardboard if you want!

Toss in some glitter!

Apply hot glue to the cardboard (painted side) 1/4" in from the edge, along the mark you traced.

Press the cardboard, hot glued side down, onto the rim of the acrylic.

You can reinforce the bond with metallic tape if needed.

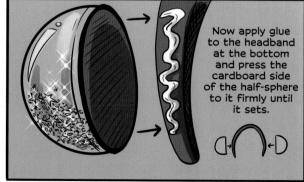

Now apply glue to the headband at the bottom and press the cardboard side of the half-sphere to it firmly until it sets.

Sparkly!

You can also paint the insides of half spheres with acrylic paint to create the pupil and iris for eyes, or patterns to create large gems. This option is great if you want big, cartoony eyes on your alien!

# MONSTER

Take a cardboard box that fits nicely over your head and cut an opening for you to see through. Or you can build a base for your mask with the same method used on the superhero pouch.

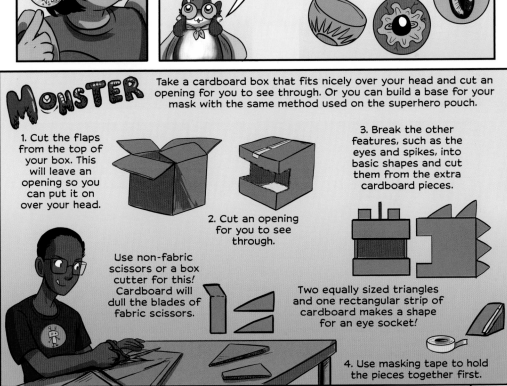

1. Cut the flaps from the top of your box. This will leave an opening so you can put it on over your head.

2. Cut an opening for you to see through.

Use non-fabric scissors or a box cutter for this! Cardboard will dull the blades of fabric scissors.

3. Break the other features, such as the eyes and spikes, into basic shapes and cut them from the extra cardboard pieces.

Two equally sized triangles and one rectangular strip of cardboard makes a shape for an eye socket!

4. Use masking tape to hold the pieces together first.

duct tape

Once you've got the basic pieces assembled for your monster head, add the eyes and spikes to the head. Use duct tape to reinforce areas you're settled on!

Extending the tape over the edges and corners helps strengthen the cardboard box's structure.

Apply tape over the edges where you can see inside the cardboard to the corrugated ridges, too.

Build up portions for the snout and eyes with cardboard.

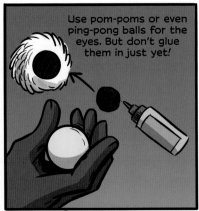

Use pom-poms or even ping-pong balls for the eyes. But don't glue them in just yet!

Leave enough room for the eyes to be placed in the eye sockets later!

Make a lower eyelid out of cardboard and tape it around the eye as a placeholder.

Here are some ideas for variations in spike and snout shapes!

classic giant monster or Kaiju spikes, but simplified

Maybe your monster is sweet.

B

A (x2)

basic rounded snout

A

B

A

A

B

Snouts can be thought of as side and top pieces.

The key is to think of these forms as simple shapes and build them up from there!
Rawr.

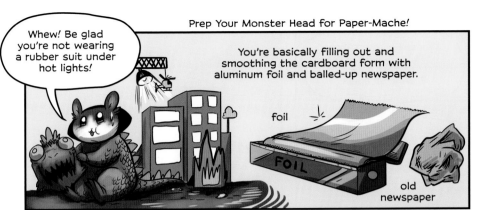

Whew! *Be glad you're not wearing a rubber suit under hot lights!*

You're basically filling out and smoothing the cardboard form with aluminum foil and balled-up newspaper.

foil

old newspaper

Build up areas you want to be smooth or rounded with newspaper or foil balls. Then tape it and cover with foil to secure it.

Tape the cover layer of foil down, too!

Think about *shape*.

Don't worry if it looks a little rough. As long as you're happy with the shape, that's all that matters right now. You'll cover this with paper-mache next.

Cut strips of old newspaper and prepare your work surface by laying down a trash bag or drop cloth or newspaper in a garage, basement, or outdoors.

Remember the super-strong paper-mache recipe from page 57? Brew it up again!

Dip the paper strips into the paper-mache...

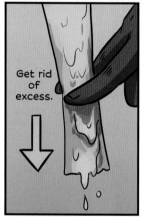

Get rid of excess.

Lay the paper strips on your monster head over your foil layer.

Smooth it down with your fingers as you go.

But be careful, because it's still as messy as ever.

It may take a couple of extra layers to get the more complicated areas smooth, such as the eyes and the snout!

You can also use balled-up paper strips wetted in the paper-mache to create things like raised nostrils! Just place another couple of layers of paper strips over the top to secure them.

Place the eyeballs in the eye sockets. Push them in while the paper-mache is still wet so they make a nice indentation and fit tightly. When it dries, you can pop them out and properly secure them with hot glue.

Let the head sit to dry undisturbed overnight in a well-ventilated, dry area.

Depending on the humidity in the air, it might take longer to dry, so allow yourself time to work on it and be patient!

Gently knock on the head to check if it is dry.

KNOCK KNOCK

Bring your monster to life!

acrylic paint

craft glue and hot glue

Now you can give your monster scales and color!

craft foam (Cut out lots of scales!)

2" wide is a good size!

glitter

Glue the scales in place.

If you add the scales to your monster first and *then* paint over them with acrylic paint, it creates a really cool skin texture! By gluing them first, you'll know where to paint a shadow between each scale.

Use the weathering technique on page 52 for additional shading.

highlight

shadow

Now hot glue the eyes in place!

Add foam teeth. Reinforce on the inside with duct tape!

Glitter or paint a lighter shade in these areas to create highlights.

Add red paint for blood on the teeth, if you want to make it look gruesome!

It's top-heavy.

Uh-oh!

This problem is easily solved!

Cushion foam can be found in craft and sewing stores!

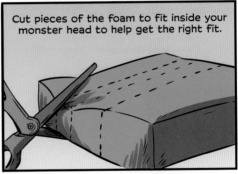

Cut pieces of the foam to fit inside your monster head to help get the right fit.

This might take some trial and error before you get the right fit. Make sure it's not too tight before gluing it into the sides of the monster head.

Hot glue craft foam scales to an old pair of gloves to make monster hands. Then add yellow triangles to the fingertips for claws!

Add more scales!

Wear the monster head with a shirt and pants in the same color.

You can use a sponge stamp with different colors of fabric paint for a layered effect. Alternate colors and stagger your pattern for rough scales.

Use a paper plate to hold your paint.

Cut your own stamp from a household sponge!

You can go as simple or complex as you want with these costumes!

You can even add spikes to the back of the shirt, just like we did the animal hoodie ears and fins!

You can do anything you can imagine with these costumes. With the skills you've learned, why not try building a squid or an octopus head? A bee? Endless possibilities!

And there are no rules about how simple or elaborate your costume should be. Let your skill, comfort level, and budget be your guide!

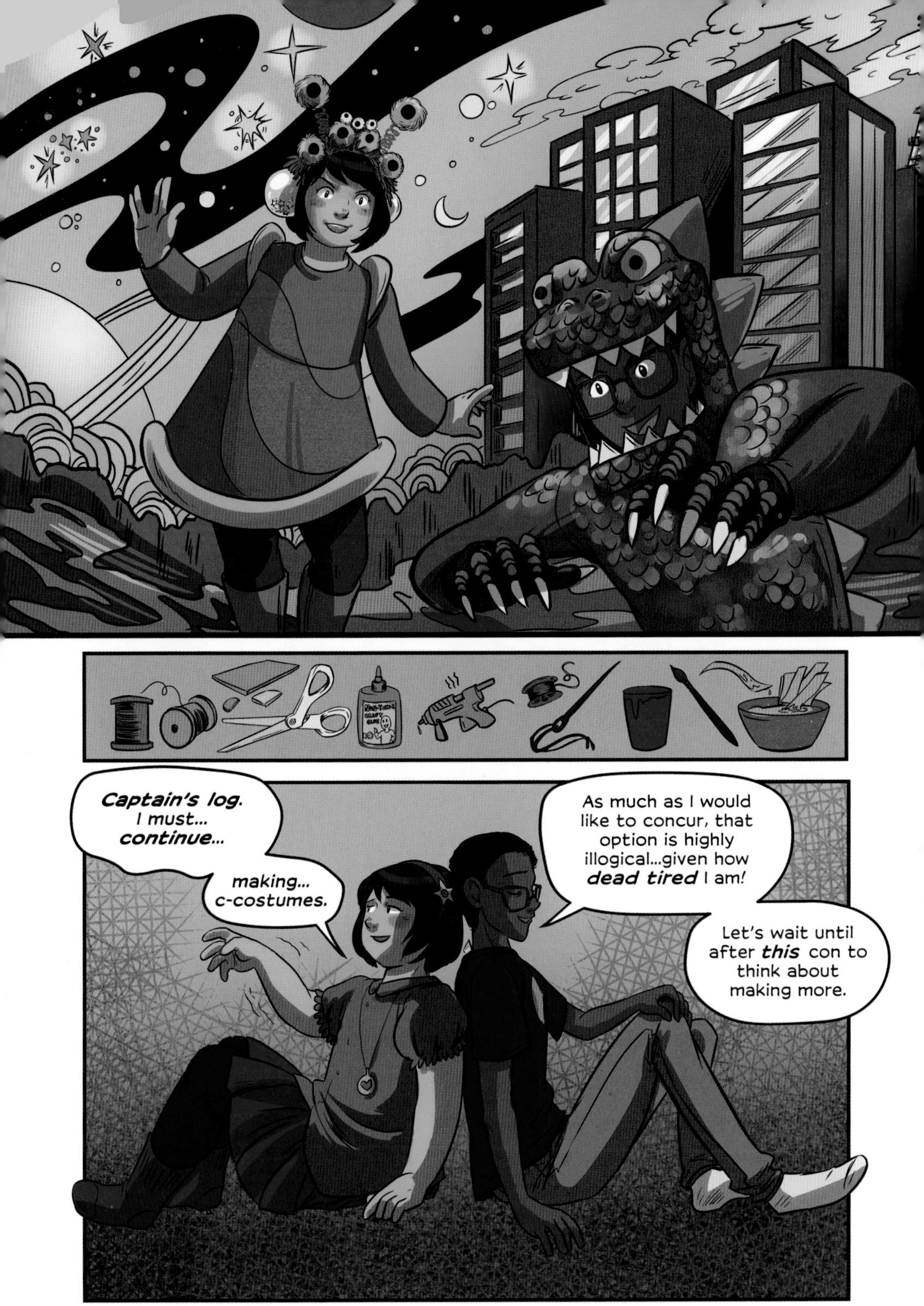
Captain's log. I must... continue...
making... c-costumes.
As much as I would like to concur, that option is highly illogical...given how dead tired I am!
Let's wait until after this con to think about making more.

# SHOW OFF!

## IT'S CONVENTION TIME!

Heyyy!

Hey! I'm *so* ready!

Okay, I've got my notes and I brought the emergency sewing kit.

Awesome. Phone?

Check.

Space costume?

Check.

First aid stuff?

Check!

Oh, and I brought my phone charger, just in case!

There they go!

The big day really came up fast, didn't it?

Making costumes for an event is just half the fun! When you wear your costume out and about, you really get to shine. Here are some helpful points to consider if you're going to a convention!

If it's your first convention, you might feel a bit overwhelmed.

*Yikes.*

*There's already a line?!*

If you're looking for registration, the line is over here!

BADGE REGISTRATION

Okay, thanks!

Excuse me! Can I get a picture?

Oh! Sure!

Yeah, okay!

It's never easy to predict what the reaction might be to a costume you make.

You might get asked by other people if they can take a photo of your costume.

Remember that it's important for you to have control of your own body.

If you don't feel comfortable with someone taking your photo, politely say no.

That's your right.
**Your body, your rules!**

I'll meet you in the food court at one o'clock, okay?

Okay, Mom! See you then!

I'm setting an alarm on my phone so we aren't late to meet my mom.

Good idea.

Hi!

Hey! You guys look amazing! Want to join our shoot?

We'd love to!

Cheese!

Oh. Hey.

You're cosplaying as Kimiko, too!

Except you did the *budget* version.

On the off chance that you run into someone who is negative or rude, don't let them get to you. Ignore them and don't engage in their bad behavior. If they continue to bother you, talk to a staff member.

If you feel that someone is crossing a line, check the convention's harassment policy.

You really *should* have—

Huh?

It's all about *respect*.

Haha! *No* way. That's the best crossover photo op ever.

Breakfast Man versus Captain Action. You won't see that again anytime soon.

Hang on a sec. Okay, I got it! Thanks, guys!

Excuse us! D'you guys mind if we pose with you for a photo?

Not at all! What do you have in mind?

Posing with other cosplayers can be one of the most enjoyable parts of conventions!

When it comes to getting photos with other cosplayers...

DO! Ask the cosplayer's permission to pose with them for photos. Wait until they are finished posing for other people before you approach them.

Respect their space if they decline or if they aren't comfortable with your pose request!

You were right about "best crossover photo op ever." I'm really getting into this!

**Don't!** Expect another person at a convention to act a certain way just because you are all wearing costumes.

Consider how you might feel if a stranger walked up to you and acted like they already knew you.

**Do!** Remember to ask permission and respect personal boundaries.

Hey! It's Mistress Mischief from issue 4! We should stage a battle with her!

I'm gonna surprise her. Get a picture!

Hold it right there!

I've got you now, *Evildoer!*

Wh-what?! Oh my g–

I-I'm...not good with... p-posing or...stuff like th-that.

I-I have to g-go...

I'm sorry I upset you.

*"Cosplay does not equal consent."*

This is another way of saying that just because someone is wearing a costume does not mean that you can touch them without permission or expect them to behave a certain way.

*No one* ever deserves to be harassed, attacked, or bullied, costume or no costume.

Everyone ready?

Okay, let's get a group shot!

Oh! I'm sorry. Why don't you stand in front?

No prob!

Thanks!

Ohhhh...wow. Is *that* what I *think* it is?

The limited edition moon baton, yep!

DO! Respect others' personal boundaries. Ask permission to handle a prop that isn't yours.

May I hold it?

Sure!

During meetups and group photo shoots, be considerate of the people around you.

Let shorter folks stand in front for photos, for example. And be respectful of personal space even when admiring another person's costume or props.

If you are thoughtful and considerate of others' personal boundaries, everyone will have a good time!

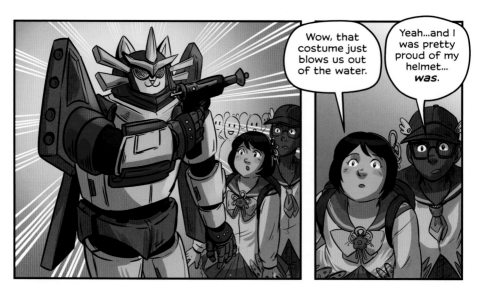

It can be easy to be overwhelmed by how many amazing costumes you see...and there will be costumes at conventions that look super impressive!

Don't let this discourage you! Instead, look at it as inspiration. Ask the cosplayer how they made it or if they have any tips or advice for you. Talk to them. Maybe they'll share some ideas with you. Be positive instead of competitive.

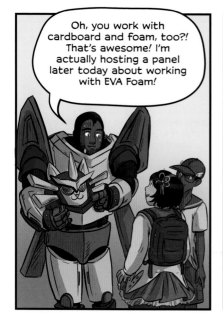

You can also attend panels about costume construction and cosplay! Not only are they informative, they are often entertaining. Learn from cosplayers you admire.

People-watch if you need a break. Don't forget to *eat*!

How's the con so far? Are you guys having a good time?

I'm pretty sure I want to *live* at conventions.

Beatrice, how did I *know* you'd say that? Hehe.

Be mindful of the people around you. Sometimes convention halls can get really crowded. Be aware of props you have or parts of your costume that stick out. If you have to walk through a tight area with lots of people, it might be a good idea to take off a helmet or headpiece that might poke people in the eye.

Watch it!

Oh! Hey, look!

Don't swing or brandish props in a threatening manner, even just in play.

Convention policies vary when it comes to props, but unless you are posing for a cosplay photo, it's best to avoid actions with your prop that could appear threatening to other convention goers. If you have questions about them, ask a convention staff member.

You might be permitted to keep your prop with you, but it might need to be peace-bonded with tape or a brightly colored ribbon for safety.

Don't wander the convention alone. Stay with a buddy and always know where your parent or guardian is at all times. If you have to split up, have a plan for where and when you will meet next.

Designate a secure place inside your costume to keep your money, phone, emergency items, etc. Keep them hidden from view.

Conventions have a friendly and fun atmosphere, because of the shared interests between people.

But it's still important to stay alert. Ultimately, you don't know everyone at the convention even if they seem friendly. They are still strangers.

*Never* give out your personal information to anyone you don't know. If you're being harassed, followed, or made to feel unsafe, find the nearest convention staff member or security guard and tell them *immediately*.

Hey, check out that *great* Mimi the Witch cosplayer!

Yeah...

She looks pretty down, though.

Excuse me!

U-uh, yeah?

I just wanted to tell you that you make a *great* Mimi!

Th-thanks!

Sometimes all it takes is one kind comment to make someone's day better.

You never know. Maybe that person wasn't feeling confident before, or had a bad day earlier, and your comment brightened their day and turned it all around.

Kindness can go a long way.

Should be about time for us to meet up with Mom!

Lead the way, Space Ranger.

It looks like they're back from the convention. Which means that it's time for a certain Costume Critter to get to sleep!

I'll bet they had a great time today.

I hope that you had fun, too. Now you're ready to make your very own costumes!

In the back of this book, you'll find a handy-dandy glossary with terms related to costume construction, cosplaying, and conventions!

I've gotten you started on making your own costumes, but you don't have to stop here! Turn to page 122 to find a list of resources for further research and inspiration as you continue making those awesome costumes. There are tons of talented cosplayers out there to learn from. As your skill level advances, you can work with more techniques and materials!

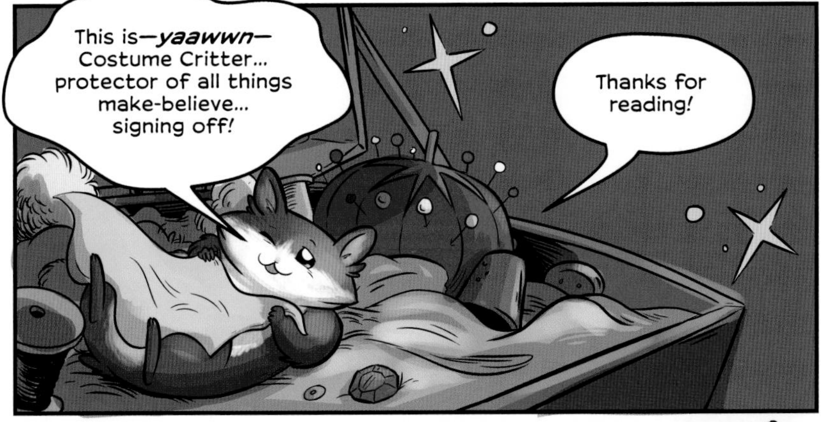
This is—*yaawwn*—
Costume Critter...
protector of all things
make-believe...
signing off!
Thanks for
reading!

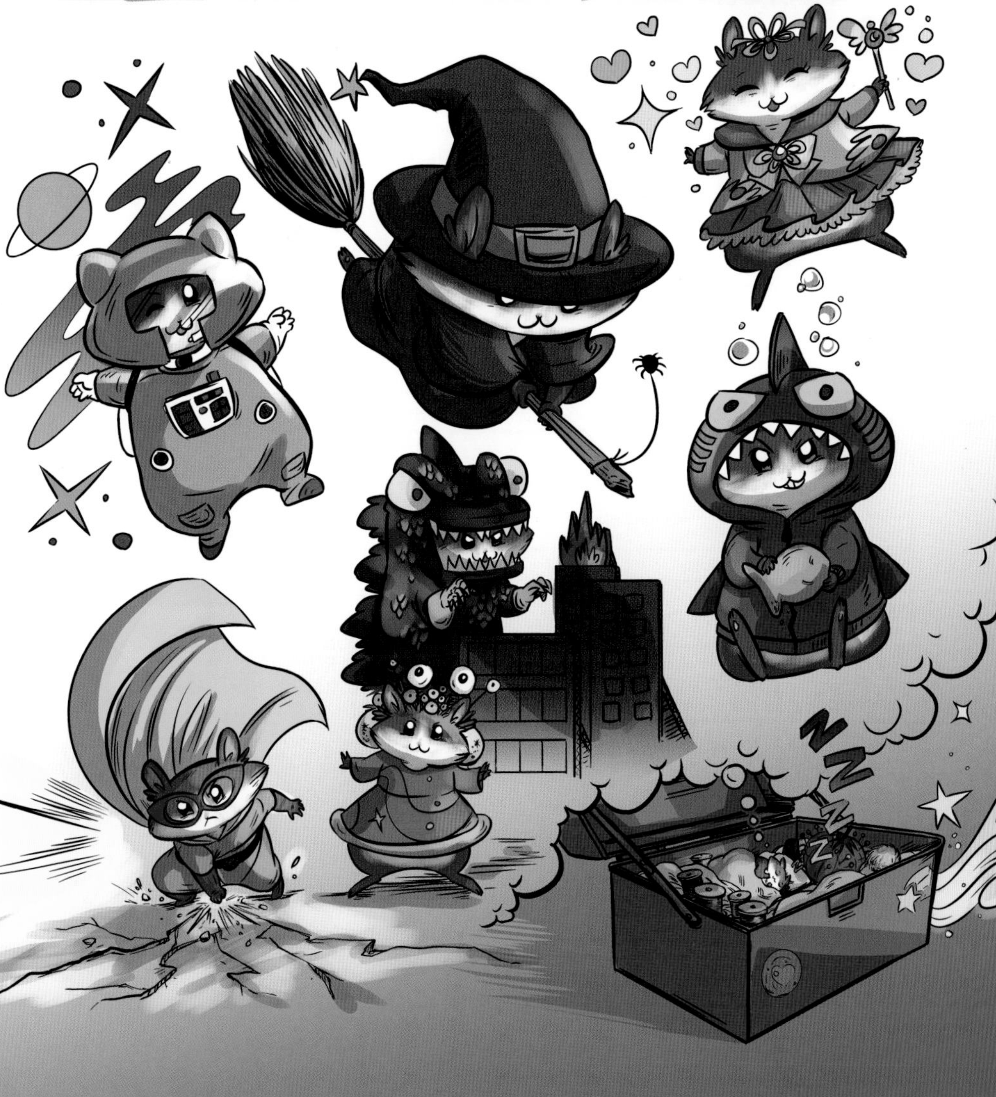
Z
Z
Z

# GLOSSARY

**bias tape** – a narrow strip of fabric with an oblique, or slanted, fabric grain that is used to bind edges of fabric or for decoration. Fabric stores sell bias tape in different sizes and in single- or double-fold thicknesses.

**cosplay** – the practice of dressing up as a character from a movie, book, or video game, especially one from the Japanese mediums of manga and anime. Can also be used to refer to the clothing or outfit.

**costuming** – to dress a person in a particular set of clothes.

**cure** – to harden (rubber, plastic, concrete, etc.) after manufacture by a chemical process such as vulcanization. Epoxy adhesives, for example, must cure in order to bond with the material to be held together.

**fabric grain** – the direction of the threads in woven fabric.

**hem** – the edge of a piece of cloth or clothing that has been turned under and sewn.

**live steel** – metal items that can potentially take an edge, not just blades or sharpened objects.

**seam** – a line along which two pieces of fabric (or other materials such as wood) are sewn together in a garment or other article.

**seam allowance** – the area between the edge and the stitching line on two (or more) pieces of material being stitched together.

**selvage** – an edge produced on woven fabric during manufacture that prevents it from unraveling.

## Conversions and Measurements

| Length Measurements | | | |
|---|---|---|---|
| 1/4" | 0.635 cm | 6.350 mm | |
| 1/2" | 1.270 cm | 12.700 mm | |
| 1" | 2.54 cm | 25.400 mm | |
| 2" | 5.08 cm | 50.800 mm | |
| 12" | 30.48 cm | 304.80 mm | 1 ft (foot) |

| Abbreviations | |
|---|---|
| in or _" | inch |
| cm | centimeter |
| mm | millimeter |
| fl oz | fluid ounce |
| ml | milliliter |

| Liquid Measurements | | |
|---|---|---|
| 1 cup | 8 fl oz | 240 ml |
| 2 cups | 16 fl oz | 470 ml |

## ADDITIONAL RESOURCES

Cosplay by McCALL's – cosplay.mccall.com
Cosplay dot com – cosplay.com
ACParadise – acparadise.com
Convention Scene – conventionscene.com
Replica Prop Forum (The RPF) – therpf.com

# GET TO KNOW YOUR UNIVERSE!

# SCIENCE COMICS

"An excellent addition to school and classroom libraries."
—*School Library Journal*

**CORAL REEFS**
*Cities of the Ocean*
MARIS WICKS

**DINOSAURS**
*Fossils and Feathers*
MK REED   JOE FLOOD

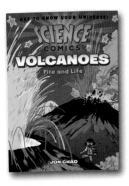

**VOLCANOES**
*Fire and Life*
JON CHAD

**BATS**
*Learning to Fly*
FALYNN KOCH

**FLYING MACHINES**
*How the Wright Brothers Soared*
ALISON WILGUS   MOLLY BROOKS

**PLAGUES**
*The Microscopic Battlefield*
FALYNN KOCH

**DOGS**
*From Predator to Protector*
ANDY HIRSCH

**ROBOTS AND DRONES**
*Past, Present, and Future*
MAIRGHREAD SCOTT   JACOB CHABOT

**SHARKS**
*Nature's Perfect Hunter*
JOE FLOOD

**ROCKETS**
*Defying Gravity*
ANNE DROZD   JERZY DROZD

**TREES**
*Kings of the Forest*
ANDY HIRSCH

**THE BRAIN**
*The Ultimate Thinking Machine*
TORY WOOLLCOTT   ALEX GRAUDINS

**SOLAR SYSTEM**
*Our Place in Space*
ROSEMARY MOSCO   JON CHAD

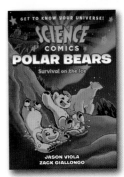

**POLAR BEARS**
*Survival on the Ice*
JASON VIOLA   ZACK GIALLONGO

**...And more books coming soon!**

First Second

Published by First Second
First Second is an imprint of Roaring Brook Press,
a division of Holtzbrinck Publishing Holdings Limited Partnership
120 Broadway, New York, NY 10271
All rights reserved

Don't miss your next favorite book from First Second! For the latest updates go to firstsecondnewsletter.com and sign up for our enewsletter.

Library of Congress Control Number: 2018944907

Paperback ISBN: 978-1-250-15208-4
Hardcover ISBN: 978-1-250-15207-7

Our books may be purchased in bulk for promotional, educational, or business use. Please contact your local bookseller or the Macmillan Corporate and Premium Sales Department at (800) 221-7945 ext. 5442 or by email at MacmillanSpecialMarkets@macmillan.com.

First edition, 2019
Edited by Robyn Chapman and Bethany Bryan
Expert consultation by Mia Moore
Book design by Rob Steen

Penciled and inked with a variable weight digital brush in Photoshop. Colored digitally in Manga Studio.

Printed in China by 1010 Printing International Limited, North Point, Hong Kong

Paperback: 10 9 8 7 6 5 4 3 2 1
Hardcover: 10 9 8 7 6 5 4 3 2 1